D1430714

FOR GOD, IT'S ALL ABOUT RELATIONSHIP

BY DAPHNE CHICK

xulon PRESS

For God, It's All About Relationship
by Daphne Chick

Printed in the United States of America

ISBN 9781626978461

www.xulonpress.com

Table of Contents

FOREWORD

"I would rather be a doorkeeper in the house of my God, than dwell in the tents of wickedness", the sons of Korah declared in Psalm 84:10. At the time these words were written there were other positions available to the people of God. Today, however, none of us can be anything but a doorkeeper. Jesus has done all the work as High Priest, and the work is finished. Our highest position is a doorkeeper. Our words as well as our lives can open the door for others to behold the beauty of the Lord and accept His Grand Invitation to a Relationship. My highest goal in this book is to be a good doorkeeper; to somehow swing the door a little wider for all who love the Lord and hunger for more of His sweet and real presence.

For God, It Is All About Relationship

As I wandered the back streets of the pueblos of Mexico, preaching the gospel to the poor and praying with so many open hearts, I shared a tract I wrote. It is written like a quiz, with scoring boxes after each question and a place at the bottom to write the total score. The heading says: "Which one do you have—Religion or Relationship?" A series of three questions followed which helped the reader arrive at a score and determine if he or she had Religion or Relationship:

Do you:

1. a) attend church as an obligation, or

   b) want to worship the Lord and love to learn His Word?

2. a) have a Bible, but have little interest in it, or

   b) crave to read His Word and hear from God?

3. a) pray in church with words you hear others say and pray your hardest only when you are in trouble, or

   b) have a personal prayer life and pour out your heart to the Lord and share everything with Him?

The tract was amazingly popular with the people. They liked the idea of finding an answer, and it opened hearts in an amenable way. Many interesting conversations proceeded from that simple tract. I never talked about a church; I only spoke about having a deeply personal and powerful Relationship with the Lord. I have found that even the simplest soul craves the satisfaction of a warm, loving relationship – they just don't know it's possible with God Himself.

As I taught again and again from the tract, its profound message began to work on my own soul. I discovered a subterranean river flowing from the very throne of God. In the sweet waters of that river I found clarity about the stunning beauty of the difference between law and grace— or Religion and Relationship. The age-old tension between law and grace is in every fiber of the Word of God. Why would God put so much in His Holy Book, specifically in the New Testament, about law and grace? Why do we have books like Hebrews, Romans, and Galatians, solely devoted to issues about Jewish Law? The first century believers were under the law; they needed to see the difference. But do *WE* need to study so much about law and grace? Apparently, yes. It is really about the complete contrast and disparity between Religion and Relationship; and they are not just different planets, they are different galaxies.

To travel from one galaxy to another takes light years. A light year is approximately 6 trillion miles and our closest galaxy is 42,000 light years away. That distance is unimaginably far. However, although Religion and Relationship are two different entities and are light years away in the spiritual realm, they can live dangerously close to one another in our souls. Consider the following passage from Isaiah chapter one:

> **11** "What makes you think I want all your sacrifices?" says

> the LORD. "I am sick of your burnt offerings of rams and the fat of fattened cattle. I get no pleasure from the blood of bulls and lambs and goats.
> **12** When you come to worship me, who asked you to parade through my courts with all your ceremony?
> **13** Stop bringing me your meaningless gifts; the incense of your offerings disgusts me! As for your celebrations of the new moon and the Sabbath and your special days for fasting—they are all sinful and false. I want no more of your pious meetings.
> **14** I hate your new moon celebrations and your annual festivals. They are a burden to me. I cannot stand them!

These had to be painful and even confusing words for the worshippers of Isaiah's day. It was God who instituted burnt offerings, incense, gifts, celebrations of the New Moon and the Sabbath, and annual festivals. Moses got holy instructions directly from God to establish all their ceremonies of worship. And yet God sent Isaiah to tell them that He now "hated" the ceremonies and that the offerings were "disgusting". The Lord says that He had "no pleasure in their offerings" which at one time He called a "sweet savor" and "holy". What happened? Quite simply, the heart was gone and they had traveled to the other galaxy – Religion.

God has given His church certain ceremonies to do as we gather: we take the Lord's Supper, or water baptize, we preach the Word and we sing songs. However, water baptism can mean nothing if it is merely a ceremony. A young man once said to me, "I went down a dry sinner and came up a wet sinner; it meant nothing to me". The taking of communion can be completely meaningless without any contemplation of the blood and body of our Lord. These words from I Corinthians 11 are more serious to Christians than Isaiah's words to the worshippers of his day:

> **27** So anyone who eats this bread or drinks this cup of the Lord unworthily is guilty of sinning against the body and blood of the Lord. **28** That is why you should examine yourself before eating the bread and drinking the cup. **29** For if you eat the bread or drink the cup without

> honoring the body of Christ, you are eating and drinking God's judgment upon yourself. **30** That is why many of you are weak and sick and some have even died.

These are strong words. Eating the bread and drinking the Lord's cup "unworthily" has been used to intimidate people about sin in their lives. However, in context "unworthily" appears to mean in a hurried and careless manner. Apparently, the end result of such a cavalier or heartless attitude will quite possibly be sickness and death! The warning in I Corinthians makes Isaiah's words appear rather tame. Every believer has slipped into heartless singing and apathetic attention to the Word. However, the rather flippant "Oh well, it happens to everybody" does not mean much to God. He is *always* in search of our hearts, every day, in every circumstance, at all times.

Chapter One

God Is All About Relationship

God has relentlessly pursued Relationship since the sixth morning of creation. That was the day He picked up a handful of dust and made the momentous and costly decision to make a person who was like Him and able to share love with Him. However, man chose to rebel and leave Relationship. Since then he gropes and hunts for Religion to try to fill the need for God without the dependency, submission and surrender of Relationship. Trying to fill the void, he has become very skilled at building a world of religious activity and avoiding the effort of Relationship.

That God, the Lord of all, craves and longs for, unto death, a relationship with man is a mystery to me. I have read and heard comments about how we were made in His image and therefore He will always be connected to us, but I still find it completely mysterious. His commitment seems inordinate, excessive, unreasonable, and certainly overpriced. Even when we were on the very brink of total destruction, when the Lord said "I am sorry I ever made man" (Gen. 6:6), the Lord extended grace seemingly at the last second: "But Noah found grace in the eyes of the Lord". Surely this is one of the most momentous verses in all of scripture. (Gen. 6:8) It is as if He couldn't let us go; no matter how grieved, or how angry He was. He just could not let us go.

Why? I connect deeply with David's cry:

> **3** When I look at the night sky and see the work of your fingers—the moon and the stars you set in place—**4** what are mere mortals that you should think about them,human beings that you should care for them? (Ps. 8:3,4)

I understand why David never answered the question. There is no real answer. God is hopelessly, helplessly connected to and in love with man. The only real answer is that it is about something in Him, because we know it is not in us.

David's life provides a window into God's focus on and commitment to Relationship. Lingering for long hours on the hills of Bethlehem with flocks of sheep, David found something. He found the "treasure hidden in a field" Jesus told about in Matthew 13:44. He found something so deep and so vast it eternally touched the heart of God. As he spent hours singing to the Lord and fellowshipping with Him, all alone, he entered into what the Lord always had in mind for mankind: a real and meaningful Relationship. As a result of hours spent with the Lord, David also became a mighty man of faith. One of the wonderful results of a close Relationship with the Lord is the comfort of having things in proper proportion. When we spend time with the Lord He gets big, powerful and magnificent, and we become small and weak and dependent.

David's hours alone with God in the hills of Bethlehem manifested in his life in a powerful way. At one point, David pulls back the curtain for us to reveal his strong Relationship with the Lord. When Saul refuses to allow David to go up against the giant Philistine who was terrorizing the armies of Israel, David, a boy of about 17 years, reveals a little of his secret life out there alone in the hills:

> "I have been taking care of my father's sheep," he said. "When a lion or a bear comes to steal a lamb from the flock, I go after it with a club and take the lamb from its mouth. If the animal turns on me, I catch it by the jaw and club it to death. I have done this to both lions and bears, and I'll do it to this pagan Philistine, for he has defied the armies of the Living God." (I Sam. 17:34-36)

What was going on out there in those hills that David was running after bears and lions, clubbing them to death? He wasn't Samson with a special gift of supernatural strength. How did the little shepherd boy became so bold? Where did he get that kind of fearlessness and strength? David had been in the presence of the Lord. He had been enjoying real Relationship, where God is so big and we are so weak. He further reveals what was going on through his wonderful words to the giant, Goliath.

> "You come to me with sword, spear, and javelin, but I come to you in the Name of the Lord Almighty – the God of the armies of Israel, whom you have defied. Today the Lord will conquer you..." (I Sam. 17: 45, 46)

How big was David's God? Absolutely huge. And how insignificant had he become? David didn't even see himself in the battle at all; this was between Goliath and God. In David's eyes Goliath was a fleck of dust compared to the great big God David had been worshipping. David had been in an intimate Relationship with the Lord, literally getting lost in Him. Serious time in His presence will always result in a clearer look at His grandeur, His greatness, and His mighty power. The more private and personal time we spend with the Lord, the bigger He becomes and the smaller we become. In fact, everything becomes smaller in His presence. All the giants assume their proper proportion.

David also pulls back the curtain for us through the beauty of the Psalms which reflect his profound relationship with God. Even by some of the most Pentecostal or Charismatic standards, David would be considered quite eccentric as he called out to the angels, the sun, moon and stars, mountains, hills and trees and told them to praise the Lord! (Psalm 148) Although the authorship of the last set of Psalms is not specifically indicated, David is generally considered to be the writer of these intense songs of selfless, ecstatic praise. David cried in Psalm 149, "Let the saints be joyful in glory, let them sing aloud upon their beds." Before David ever wrote those words to all the saints, we can be sure that he himself shouted and wept in the presence of God while lying on his own bed at night.

Later in David's life, he lost his grip on the wonder, the power and the sweetness of that sacred Relationship and he set a lustful eye on someone he thought for a moment could fill that empty place – Bathsheba. So distant was his heart from the Lord that David even resorted to murder to cover his sin. Murder and adultery! How heinous and despicable for a man of God. However, one generation later God warned Solomon to "walk before Me as David thy father walked in integrity of heart and in uprightness..." (I KI. 9:4 KJV) And to Jeroboam, the next generation, God sent a prophet to tell of the coming disaster because he had not walked in the Lord's ways and he did not keep His statutes "as did David his father." (I KI. 11:33) Later, the prophet sent the word of the Lord to Jeroboam telling him that he had "not been as my servant David, who kept my commandments and who followed me with all his heart to do that only which was right in my eyes." (I KI 14:8 KJV)

What? Does God have some sort of memory loss here? Has He forgotten David's heinous sin? How could God say that David kept His commandments and followed the Lord with all his heart? Scripture honors David in amazing ways. One astounding fact that seems to supremely honor David in an unimaginable way is recorded in the prophets: in the Millennium, when the earth is restored and the glory of the Lord covers the whole earth, Jesus will sit on what scripture calls, the "throne of David". (Isa. 9:6, 7)

All of these verses, and many others, show amazing honor for a little shepherd boy turned king, a hero turned sinner. In the New Testament the Lord testifies of David: "I have found David the son of Jesse, a man after my own heart..." (Acts 13:22) David had deeply connected with the heart of God. He entered into real Relationship. He found the key to the heart of God. There is no sure interpretation for the "key of David" in the hand of the resurrected Christ in Revelation 3:7, however, an application can be made. David indeed found a key to the very heartbeat of God. God has heaped honor on His servant David who cried,

> "As the deer pants after the water brooks, so pants my soul after thee, O God. My soul thirsts for God, for the Living God...", and "My soul longs, yea, even faints for the courts of the Lord: my heart and my flesh cry out for the Living God". (Psalm 42:1, Psalm 84:2 KJV)

David's deep soul hunger to be in God's presence mirrors the very hunger of God who redeemed us not just to go to heaven, but for Relationship, both in this life and the next one.

It is not that David's sin and disobedience didn't matter to God because he drew so close; David was punished severely for his sin. Obedience is a critical facet of our love relationship; our songs and praises mean very little to God if we are disobedient. But God never forgot those sweet days when the shepherd boy sat on the hills of Bethlehem and sang, prayed and wept his way into the heart of God. Even when times got tough, David continued in his loving relationship as he ran from cave to cave through years of persecution by Saul. David wrote Psalms while he sat in those dark caves and he learned to praise and worship God in the worst of circumstances. For ten long years, David was in a situation that is actually quite conducive to finding sweet fellowship with the Lord: the situation was completely unfair and it was accompanied by painfully uncomfortable conditions. Often, we miss our own handcrafted opportunity to find Him in such conditions, but it is the perfect setting. The cave of *unfair* and *uncomfortable* is actually a holy sanctuary. Just ask David, the man after God's own heart with a key in his hand.

Chapter 2

Religion Is Easy – Relationship Is Hard

The ungodly leader of the Communist movement, Karl Marx, wrote this famous quote: "Religion is the opiate of the masses" (Marx, 1843). Karl Marx meant to be critical of Christianity but, in fact, the statement is true. Man is a religious creature, not because he wants a relationship with God, but because he wants to fill the void of being estranged from his Creator and he wants to fill it with something *he makes* and something *he can control.* Cultures around the world have created bizarre and dark religious practices; worshipping snakes, cows, planets and even demons, and everywhere religion is found it is an opiate. It is indeed an enchanting drug. People get stirred and they hallucinate and "feel" that they have found the gods. They vainly imagine that they have filled the space in the human heart made only for a Relationship with God.

But opium has another effect besides euphoria and hallucinations: it puts people in a half awake/half asleep state. Religion is a sedative; it puts people in a sleepy condition, and the drive to seek after God gets lost. Religion dulls the senses to the sweet voice of God and it eclipses the need for intimate fellowship with the Lord. Religion gives the participant a false sense of God and, like the opiate, it yields a rather convincing hallucination that since we are faithful in our dutiful study or church attendance, all is well with the Lord. Religion, therefore, shuts the door to Relationship and keeps people asleep to the vital and powerful walk in the Spirit, and closeness to the Lord.

Our human nature seeks refuge in Religion. It is the ultimate hide-out if we are caught in the deceitful world of believing in Christ as Savior but not surrendering to Him as Lord. Once we are a true follower of the Lord Jesus Christ we won't seek refuge in the bars, or in drugs or in affairs. And as we more fully dedicate ourselves to God, we may rid ourselves of other places for our will to stay in control: too much work, food, busyness, shopping, entertainments, etc. But, ultimately, the last hideout where our unsurrendered hearts will want to hide from the beautiful but crucifying life of real intimacy with God will be —- Religion. Religion is the **perfect** hideout. We can be very committed; we can be faithful, giving and helpful, and yet our self-life can stay alive. With all our hard religious work we may acquire a false sense of satisfaction, believing we have Relationship. But in reality, we don't get much of the presence of the Lord; we basically end up with the frustration and emptiness of Religion.

Religion can be pretty satisfying. Billions of people enjoy it regularly. Buddhists, Catholics, Taoists, Hindus, Moslems, and Christians thrive on it. A certain sense of satisfaction is achieved by both burning incense to the gods AND by attending a church service, singing a few songs, listening to a sermon and saying hello to some nice people. And here is the scary truth: all Christian activities can be done **without** Relationship. God is faithful and is present in any gathering where the Name of Jesus Christ is honored, but millions attend church, read the Bible, volunteer to help and never enter into real and intimate Relationship with God.

There is NOTHING harder in this world than relationship. It is everyone's ultimate test. The availability of Marriage and Family Conferences, counseling, books, tapes, seminars and DVD's about making our relationships work, all attest to the difficulty of relationships. Relationship with the Lord is also hard. No one likes to admit it, but it is true; it is very difficult. And we need to candidly look at the difficulties.

DIFFICULTY# 1

First of all, there is the obvious: we can't see Him or touch Him with our natural senses. In the beginning of our journey into Relationship this is somewhat of an obstacle. However, as we spend time with the Lord and get to know His touch and His voice, that hurdle will be completely overcome. In fact, we will begin to long for the special sweetness of His spiritual touch and His gentle voice. But it takes time – it just takes time. But it is time well invested.

Jesus gave us some insight to that special delight of believing without seeing through His disciple, Thomas. When the disciples had seen the Lord after His resurrection, he was not with the group. Thomas stated to the others that he would not believe unless he could personally touch the nail wounds in Jesus' hands and touch His pierced side.

Eight days later, after Thomas blurted out those bold words, Jesus again appeared to the disciples and walked up to Thomas and said, "Put your finger here and see My hands and put your hand in my side." Thomas was stunned, and cried out "My Lord and my God!" Jesus then let him know that as magnificent as it was to actually touch those wonderful scars, there was a greater blessing for those who would never see or touch, and yet believe. He told him, "You believe because you have seen me. Blessed are those who haven't seen me and believe anyway." (Jn. 20:29) As our Relationship with the Lord matures we will find that there is a certain blessedness in walking by faith and not by sight.

> "You love Him even though you have never seen Him. Though you do not see Him, you trust Him; and even now you are happy with a glorious, inexpressible joy." (I Peter 1:8)

Walking with and trusting Him who we cannot see brings a certain inexpressible joy. The heart experiences insight and intimacy that goes beyond our senses. The more time we spend with the Lord, the more real His spiritual touch and voice will be.

This is only one obstacle, but there are other others. It is important to recognize the difficulties in our relationship with the Lord, just as it is important to openly discuss problems within a family or any important relationship. Actually, it is more important as no relationship in our lives is as important as our Relationship with God.

DIFFICULTY #2:

A Relationship with God is difficult because His values differ so much from ours, and He is perfect. If He weren't perfect we could try to change His values, but He cannot be moved. His value system and priorities are not negotiable.

The values issue is huge. We value things like security, comfort, and consistency. He values transformation of our character which will always involve discomfort, change, and leaps of faith off cliffs with no parachute. This is a big obstacle between us and God. Even if our conscious mind doesn't know it, our human nature knows this difference in purpose and goals exists. We hide from the terrifying prospect of a close relationship with Someone whose values directly conflict with ours – and who is inflexible. So instead of "panting after

God like the deer after the water brooks" we become like the lizard who lives in my garden next to the front steps. He sticks his head out into the sun as long as I am perfectly still sitting on my front steps. But as soon as I make a move – any move – he darts back into his safe little hiding place. We may launch out a little into a closer Relationship, but when God makes a move, often we dart back into the risk free zone of Religion. It's so much safer in Religion. We can control it; we can be sure of how it will all work out. Bible study will be at 7pm, we volunteer on Saturday, and Sunday the service will go exactly like it should go, with maybe a little joke or slip-up here or there to make it just a little different from last week.

There is no way to overcome the obstacle of difference in values. He is the Lord and He is running the universe with His purposes, His goals, and His plan. There will be no negotiations.

There is an answer to this dilemma. Actually, there are two answers. The first answer revolves around the fact that He is perfect. This means His choices and His handcrafted circumstances of difficulty are also perfect. John, the young man so secure in his relationship he called himself, "the disciple whom Jesus loved," wrote three powerful letters. John's first letter begins with this massive overarching declaration in chapter one:

> **5** This is the message we heard from Jesus and now declare to you: God is light, and there is no darkness in him at all.

AT ALL are important words. The dilemma is gone! We can trust Him. Shout it from the housetops! WE CAN TRUST HIM! No darkness at all. Pure Goodness!

You really don't have much of a relationship with someone you don't trust. You may be friendly with that person, but you will never open your heart. A close relationship with the Lord is terrifying to our human nature. Our human nature cringes at the prospect of being close to God because it's true: when we get close, He *will* tear into our secret places of self-preservation, pride, and control, but **WE CAN TRUST HIM**. It will actually be a great relief to let go of our selfish world and surrender to His world of transformation. If we don't completely trust the Hands of the Potter to shape our lives any way He wants, with whatever tool He chooses, we will never draw close into a joyful, rewarding, intimate Relationship.

The second answer to the conflict of goals is that we must value closeness with the Lord above our differences. We know "the Lord's ways are not our ways" and that "as high as the heavens are above the earth, so are His ways higher than ours."(Isa. 55:8,9) His ways are mysterious and unfathomable, but He will not change. However, if we desire Him, and want His voice and His touch in our lives, the differences will become insignificant. We were created for close fellowship with the Lord. When we finally leave the world of Religion and go to Relationship, we will find the home we have longed for all of our lives.

DIFFICULTY #3:

Another reason why Relationship with the Lord is difficult is that we normally want very little to do with solitude. While teaching on prayer Jesus said, "When you pray, go into your closet and shut the door."(Matt. 6:6) We hardly know what to do with solitude. Busyness is a serious addiction in the American culture, and seems to be built into our DNA. If the Pastor asks for volunteers to come to the church at six o'clock to arrange tables and chairs and set up for a big dinner, volunteers are everywhere. If he asks for volunteers to come to find a quiet place for an hour and pray and meditate on the Lord and His Word, he'll find precious few. What a supreme tragedy! That some would prefer to set up tables and chairs over an hour of sweet fellowship with the Lord is a transgression against the Plan of the Ages, the purpose of God's sacrifice. The purpose of the cross was reconciliation of a broken Relationship, not getting our doctrine straight and attending a nice church.

Solitude, shutting ourselves away with the Lord, and closing the door on the phone calls, email, and chores, and just sitting with the Lord is one of the most sacred and life changing experiences we can have. He has wonderful experiences awaiting those who obey His words, "Go into your closet and shut the door." It is not easy to shut out the world and close the door on the need to be doing something. I lived in a beautiful house on 40 isolated acres in a small town in Colorado. There was 100 miles of National Forest behind me and 200 acres of open prairie between me and a very distant paved road. There was not another house or even a barn in sight.

Through letting some past conflicts disturb me, I had slowly let go of Relationship and, without knowing it, I had slipped into

Religion. I was attending church, teaching the Bible, and volunteering for everything, but real intimacy with the Lord had all but perished. The hunger in my heart began to ache. I grieved with a sense of deep loss. I missed Him; I needed Him; I desperately wanted my Relationship back. I paced through my house, where I had such perfect solitude, and I wept and prayed and praised. I sat in the courtyard and talked from my heart. I sat in my office where I could see the magnificent 14,000 foot peaks, and poured my soul out to my Father. But I began to realize a pattern: if I was in the main part of the house, I would eventually see a pile of mail I needed to sort through; if I was in the courtyard, I would see the weeds growing in between the bricks, and my office was littered with work to be done. I began to realize that if I was going to restore my intimacy with God I was going to have to do it His way: I needed a prayer closet. I found my spot in the bathroom by the bathtub. Facing west I couldn't see any shoes that needed to be put away or smeared toothpaste on a drawer. It was perfect. Almost. Then one day the phone rang and I realized the world could still find me, and finally I obeyed the Lord's exact instructions and I SHUT THE DOOR. Once I fully complied with His directive, I found sweet fellowship, the sound of His voice, and the nearness I was longing for. Solitude is not easy to find. You must fight for it, and then battle to keep it. But the reward is beyond description.

DIFFICULTY #4:

The Lord has an odd propensity for silence. I hate the silent treatment. At times, I would rather have yelling and screaming than cold silence. "Silence is golden" the old saying goes, and it is golden when it means peacefulness. I love living in places where I cannot hear any sounds of the spinning pace of life at all; I can hear His voice and find Him in silence. But when **He** is silent, it is painful because He seems to be somewhat distant, or even absent. But this is a very real part of having a Relationship with God; He gets distant. David experienced this aspect of Relationship. In Psa. 10:1 he cries, "Why do you stand afar off, O Lord? Why do you hide yourself in times of trouble?" And in Psalm 13:1 David cries, "How long will you forget me, O Lord? forever? How long will you hide your face from me?" This dilemma is, in part, due to the difference in values. We value ease; He values difficulty. We value now; He values eternity. We value knowing; He values trust.

One verse of Scripture addresses the dilemma of a distant God who, as David says, stands afar off and hides: "You shall seek Me and find Me when you search for Me with all of your heart." (Jeremiah 29:13) The Lord is very giving; He has shared with us His own Son and his home in eternity, but when it comes to our hearts and our attention – He doesn't share. His standing afar off is often a response to our own half-heartedness. The Lord hates lukewarm. In fact, this condition of neither hot nor cold inspires a startling response from our passionate God. Scripture tells us that lukewarm, part hot and part cold, will be spit out of His mouth. (Rev. 3:16) God is very jealous of our affections. In Exodus 34:14 He calls Himself by the name Jealous. If our attention is divided, if we are thinking about other things and dutifully doing our quiet time with thoughts elsewhere, we may well find an absent, silent God. When we want that wonderful Relationship more than anything else, when we crave it, long for it, and are desperate for it, we *will* find HIM. It's a promise.

"Lord, teach us to pray, just as John taught his disciples", one of His disciples requested after watching Jesus at prayer. (Lk. 11:1) Jesus answered directly and gave the framework we have called "The Lord's

Prayer", which has been so misused through the centuries by Religion. But after giving the template of the prayer, Jesus told a story in Luke 11. "Then teaching more about prayer, He used this illustration." He asked them to imagine that they had gone to a friend's house at midnight to ask for some bread. But their friend called from his bed and said, "Don't bother me, the door is locked for the night, we are all in bed, I can't help you." Then Jesus stopped His hypothetical story and said:

> "Even though He won't get up because of your friendship, if you keep knocking long enough, he will get up and give you some bread." Jesus continued: "And so I tell you, keep on asking and you will be given what you ask for. Keep on looking and you will find. Keep on knocking and the door will be opened." (Luke 11:1-9)

What? What are we supposed to think about the grumpy, lazy friend who won't get up? What does this mean? The story has fascinating insights into the reality of prayer. We may encounter a distant, reluctant God who is silent in our hour of need. He is not grumpy or lazy, but He can be reluctant to respond to us quickly. We may have to keep on asking, keep on seeking, and keep on knocking; He may wait until we ask, seek and knock with **all** our hearts, undistracted, undivided and passionate. He may not rise up and respond because of our official standing of sonship, but He will respond because of the pure quality of our cry; that quality of our cry is found when we cry to Him with ALL of our heart as Jeremiah 29:13 states.

The life and prayer of Manasseh, King of Judah has to be one of the foremost examples in Scripture of the all-your-heart prayer that God hears. Manasseh was the son the godly King Hezekiah. However, in spite of seeing a revival under his father's rule, Manasseh was one of the most evil kings that ever led Israel. The Scriptures tell us that he filled Jerusalem with murder and worshipped all the false gods. II Kings 21:6, 7 records:

> **6** Manasseh also sacrificed his own son in the fire. He practiced sorcery and divination, and he consulted with mediums and psychics. He did much that was evil in the LORD's sight, arousing his anger. **7** Manasseh even made

> a carved image of Asherah and set it up in the Temple, the very place where the LORD had told David and his son Solomon: "My name will be honored forever in this Temple.."

The Lord warned Manasseh through the prophets, but he would not listen. He practiced the wicked works of the heathen nations and then led God's holy people into even more malignant and atrocious sin. Finally, the Lord sent destruction and punishment to Manasseh. But the story takes an astounding turn when Manasseh gets sincere before the Lord:

> **10** The LORD spoke to Manasseh and his people, but they ignored all his warnings.**11** So the LORD sent the commanders of the Assyrian armies, and they took Manasseh prisoner. They put a ring through his nose, bound him in bronze chains, and led him away to Babylon.**12** But while in deep distress, Manasseh sought the LORD his God and sincerely humbled himself before the God of his ancestors.**13** And when he

> prayed, the LORD listened to him and was moved by his request. So the LORD brought Manasseh back to Jerusalem and to his kingdom. Then Manasseh finally realized that the LORD alone is God! (II Chron. 33)

This account of an earnest prayer has meant much to me over the years. It gives such deep hope. God hears our cry in the worst of circumstances. Manasseh returned to his throne and he cleaned up Jerusalem; he tore down all the false altars he had erected and restored true worship in the Temple. When he prayed that day in chains in a Babylonian prison, he meant business with God. Verse 19 in the II Chronicles account tells us that his prayer was recorded in a book entitled, *The Record of the Seers*, which has been lost in time. However, the fact that it was recorded at one time tells us that Manasseh told others of his history changing prayer and perhaps encouraged many to repent with his same words. But saying the right words is not what the Lord wants. He wants the right heart, and apparently, the evil and broken king Manasseh prayed a full-hearted prayer that the Lord could not resist.

DIFFICULTY #5:

A final difficulty may be summed from the words of Isaiah 55:9: "His ways are not our ways, as high above the heavens are to the earth..." That all sounds wonderful, until His completely different ways come to the doorstep of our comfortable and well-planned life. We think it's awesome how Abraham was told to leave everything comfortable and go wander around and wait for God to show him a new land, until God acts that way with us. Jesus called fishermen to leave everything and come and follow Him; these were men who had good businesses, equipment and families. We sit in Sunday School and revel in the excitement of their commitment, but deep down inside we fear this God.

This difficulty is somewhat like Difficulty #2: the danger of getting close to Someone whose values and goals differ so greatly from our own. However, this obstacle has to do with the fear of total surrender. Deep inside we may be pondering what is this God, who is so different, going to do with my life? As we draw closer we will have to surrender our will to His will. However, the journey to surrendering our will may be extremely arduous. Hidden in the internal shadows of fear, doubt, and unbelief, the heart may wonder — just exactly what might He ask me to do?

His ways with His most dedicated servants are not just different, they seem completely radical. We love the story of Daniel in the lions' den but *we* don't want to be thrown in the lion's den. We love the story of the Red Sea parting at the last second and the Israelites crossing on dry ground but *we* don't want enemies breathing down our necks at an impossible Red Sea. We love the boldness of Apostle Paul and want to be bold like him, but we don't want to say with him....

> **24** Five different times the Jewish leaders gave me thirty-nine lashes. **25** Three times I was beaten with rods. Once I was stoned. Three times I was shipwrecked. Once I spent a whole night and a day adrift at sea. **26** I have traveled on many long journeys. I have faced danger from rivers and from robbers. I have faced danger from my own people, the Jews, as well as from the Gentiles. I have faced danger in the cities, in the deserts, and on the seas. And I

> have faced danger from men who claim to be believers but are not.
> **27** I have worked hard and long, enduring many sleepless nights. I have been hungry and thirsty and have often gone without food. I have shivered in the cold, without enough clothing to keep me warm. (2 Cor. 11)

This is intimidating to people who crave predictability and things to be orderly and painless. When we get close to our Lord, who is so unpredictable and who seems to lead His best servants into lion's dens, it can produce some fear. However, it is the Lord's right to do something new and different in our lives and with our lives. He called Isaiah to walk around naked and howl; He called Ezekiel to lie on his side for 390 days and stare at a frying pan; He called Hosea to marry the town prostitute; He called Daniel to live in Babylon, and sent Joseph to slavery in Egypt. The list of unique things God has done with His surrendered servants is BIG, and so are His ideas. If we draw close, He will do some unique things in our lives. It will be thrilling and it will be exciting, but it will be something new and different. But it might feel a little unsafe.

Untold thousands stay away from an intimate and devoted relationship with God because of the fear of being called out of their comfort zone. People may have a real dissatisfaction with their lives, but they believe if they keep their own plans, at least they will still have some control. Completely surrendering to God seems like a ticket to being wildly out of control. This is a tragic and devious deception concocted by the one who loves to get us playing the endless Religion game, and away from Relationship. Ask Daniel, Moses, Paul, Abraham — are they all glad they wholly surrendered to the Lord and followed Him? We know the answer. God has a perfect plan that fits each life, and no one has ever regretted walking in the beauty of total surrender.

Chapter 3

RELIGION – WHAT IS IT?

Ultimately, all Religion is Satanic. It is created, proffered and fueled by Satan and the legions of hell. In its full manifestation, all Religion is a filthy, vile darkness. It is imperative to understand that millions will be in a dark eternity because of Religion. Mass killings and murderous wars have been initiated by Religion. Suicide bombers inflamed by Religion kill themselves and others.

The New Testament uses the word "religion" one time in James 1:26, 27:

> **26** If you claim to be religious but don't control your tongue, you are fooling yourself, and your religion is worthless. **27** Pure and genuine religion in the sight of God the Father means caring

> for orphans and widows in their distress and refusing to let the world corrupt you.

James addressed his letter to the Jewish Christians who had fled Jerusalem because of severe persecution. Many of those early believers had tried to mix their ceremonial Religion with the New Covenant of Relationship through Christ. In context, therefore, James uses the word for ceremonial religion trying to redefine what "pure and genuine religion" would look like, and it is the polar opposite of Satan's evil and twisted scheme. The record of the Fall of Lucifer recorded by the prophet Isaiah gives insight to Satan's tangled web of Religion

Sin originated with Lucifer, a fabulously beautiful and powerful angel of God (Ezek. 28, Isa. 14). Rebellion and envy began with him, and according to standard Bible interpretation, he took one-third of the angels with him into the frenzy of his attempted takeover in the heavens. In fact, when Adam, and his wife Eve, listened to Satan and transgressed God, they joined a rebellion that was already in progress.

What was at the core of Satan's Rebellion? As a prophet who can see events both in the future and the past, Isaiah gives us insight into Lucifer's heart and the reason for his rebellion.

> "How art thou fallen from heaven O Lucifer, son of the morning! ... For thou hast said in thine heart... I will exalt my throne above the stars of God; I will sit also upon the mount of the congregation"(Isa 14:12-14 KJV).

Isaiah looked back into another world, a piece of completely unknown history, and tells us the very thoughts that took root in Satan's heart. "I will sit upon the mount of the congregation", his lustful heart cried. He wanted the one thing he could not have —- worship. He wanted to be on the throne. He wanted to sit at the head of the ecstatic, heavenly singing and praising in the congregation of heaven: angels, archangels, living creatures, falling elders and whatever else God created for His good pleasure. Satan coveted that worship and he continues to crave it and pursue it above all else.

Matthew chapter four tells of a foreordained combat between the fallen angel, Lucifer, and God's Son sent to save humanity from their devastating choice to join Lucifer's Rebellion. "Jesus was led out into the wilderness by the Holy Spirit to be tempted there by the devil." This divinely orchestrated appointment between Rebel and Redeemer reveals much about the Prince of Darkness.

There He was, the lowly Son of Man in the wilderness "among the wild animals" (Mk. 1:13). He was weak from fasting for forty days and very isolated when He met Lucifer. He was face to face with the unholy angel who He had actually seen cast out of heaven (Lk 10:18). Lucifer, still driven for supremacy and glory, was given direct access to Jesus to confront him with his best fiery darts. Once again, Satan wanted to overcome God Himself, by destroying His Son.

First, Lucifer tried to lure Jesus into disobedience through food. After all, it had worked so well with Eve. He had given her a few suggestions about a higher position and Gen. 3:6 tells us "she saw the fruit was good to eat" and she ate, thereby joining Satan's Rebellion. But even after forty days and "being very hungry" Jesus declined the temptation saying, "Man shall not live by bread alone but by every word that proceeds from the mouth of God."(Matt. 4:4) With His triumph over the basic need for food, Jesus denied Satan his victory and showed us that a spiritual meal is more important than all other food.

Satan failed to entice Jesus through His appetite; he had to try something else. He used another trap that has killed many religious people: permissive, cheap, grace. Satan has taken countless people to hell with his cheap grace message of, "go ahead worship a few idols, have a little happiness with adultery and the world, God won't care, His grace will cover for you." First Corinthians 10:1-11 depicts how God's people had "tested the Lord" with their adulteries, complaining, and rebellion, and many perished. Satan, therefore, tested the Lord to do something rash and trust that His Father would cover for His foolishness. Taking Jesus to a high place, Satan encouraged Him to jump to show that the Father and the angels would rescue Him. Jesus would have none of it: "Do not tempt the Lord Thy God", solidly declining the temptation.

Finally, according to the Matthew account, Lucifer pulled out the "ace of spades" from his wicked heart and revealed what he **really** wanted. When Lucifer got the human race to join his Rebellion, he became the god of the entire world system, including politics, economics, culture, entertainments, and education. It's all his. That is why the scripture says, "Whosoever is a friend of the world is the enemy of God" (James 4:4). But Satan was willing to part with ALL of it, every bit of his power, influence, dominion, authority, and control, absolutely all of it — for what? "All these things I will give you, if you will fall down and worship me." Lucifer said to Jesus. (Matt. 4:9) There it is. He revealed the one thing that is of supreme value to him above all things. He would give EVERYTHING for it. He wants worship.

Did Satan really think the Son of God might fall to the ground and worship him? Yes, he did, or he never would have tried to cut the deal. He was willing to give up everything to "sit upon the mount of the congregation." Satan's greatest goal is direct worship; worship by the Son of God Himself would have been everything he ever wanted. But Jesus replied to his taunt, "You must worship the Lord your God and serve only Him."(Matt. 4:10) Satan failed AGAIN. He failed in heaven to gain that exalted position and he failed again with Jesus in the wilderness. He would have to find another way to get that worship his twisted soul so craves; he has never given up on his goal. Since he has failed to bask in the glory of direct praise and worship he has found a way to achieve it surreptitiously —- through Religion.

I have a friend who loves to play games; board games, charade games, dominoes, cards, whatever. She loves games. But one game in particular is her favorite. She literally squeals with delight when someone mentions that particular game. Lucifer, or Satan, is also a game player. He's got the love-of-money game, the drug game, the pornography game, the hate game, the anger game, and thousands of others. He plays them wildly like an obsessed child with thousands of clanging, whistling video games all going at once. But one game makes him squeal with delight – the Religion game. He loves it. He is at the top of his game when he gets to play Religion. He revels in it when millions offer incense, chant, dance, or spin prayer wheels, to snakes, cows, dragons, and statues. But Satan knows what true worship is, and it is true worship that he covets the most. He desires worship not filtered through idols or statues, human passions, or material acquisitions. He craves worship that is direct and personal. Therefore, his very favorite religious game is Christianity. He is never happier than when he has a Bible in his hand.

Satan knows the scripture well and loves to use it. "Beware of false prophets who are wolves in sheep's clothing," Jesus said in Matthew chapter seven. Satan loves to dress up and put on the whitest, highest gloss, dynamic, innocent looking sheep outfit he can find. He can preach, prophesy, lay hands on the sick, run denominations, sit on church boards, pastor, teach, and pray with this refined and elaborate costume. With his disguise he has gotten to "sit on the mount of the congregation." He doesn't care too much for the phony worship of playing flutes to cobras, bowing to Buddhas or spinning prayer wheels. He knows what real worship is; he saw it in the heavenly realm and he coveted it. He wants the real thing.

The Satanic imitation of Christian leaders and workers is well documented in Scripture. Apostle Paul tells us not to be surprised about it. Speaking of false apostles he says:

> "These people are false apostles. They are deceitful workers, who disguise themselves as apostles of Christ. But I am not surprised! Even Satan disguises himself as an angel of light. So it is no wonder that his servants also disguise themselves as ministers of righteousness" (II Cor. 11:13–15).

No surprise? No wonder? I've seen wolves decked out in the most fabulous, fluffy sheep's clothing with an excellent knowledge of Scripture. I still marvel. To acknowledge that someone could preach the Word and yet be driven by Satan is believable, but that the charade could go as far as becoming a "minister of righteousness" is a phenomenal freak show. But there is NO END to what Lucifer will do to "sit upon the mount of the congregation."

> "Not everyone who calls out to me, Lord, Lord, will enter the Kingdom of Heaven. Only those who actually do the will of my Father in heaven will enter. On judgment day many will say to me, Lord, Lord...... but I will reply, I never knew you." (Matt. 7:21-22)

Many? Really? Many will cry to Jesus and call Him LORD and yet will hear, "I never knew you." He's not talking about snake worshippers and Buddhists; these are people who see Him as Lord. The passage reveals that these same people have seen miracles and have preached and in Luke 13 they say "we ate and drank in your presence." Perhaps these two descriptions from Matthew 7 and Luke 13 describe deceived people who get caught in the sticky web of Religion. They are people who experienced miracles and also people who attended church suppers (ate and drank in His presence). Many of these believers in Jesus point fingers at each other. The wild antics and showmanship of supposed miracle workers are pointed at with disgust by the dutiful attendees at the church suppers. The chase-after-miracles crowds point their fingers at the "frozen chosen" and their emotionless religion. Apparently, many from every style of worship and tradition will suffer the eternal consequences of having only Religion. Those who hear the terrifying words, "I never knew you" will know that the trap of Religion kept them from what God always wanted – Relationship.

What does Satan's imitation have to do with us? Sincere Christians who want to serve God may believe that the sticky Religion trap is far away. This admonition from I Peter tells us Satan's best traps are nearby:

> "Stay alert! Watch out for your great enemy the devil. He prowls around like a roaring lion, looking for someone to devour." (I Pet. 5:8)

How is he going to devour you? He is prowling around like a cat who slinks low and silently puts one foot in front of another while staying absolutely fixed on you, the prey. What will he put before you? An affair with the neighbor? Drugs? If you are past falling for these destructive sins, he will use his refined tool, his favorite game, the game of Religion. It's a popular one. "Many" will show up in eternity with only Religion and be sent into outer darkness.

Chapter 4

Relationship – How Important Is It?

Luke 10:38 - 42 records a wonderful story with a profound message. Jesus went to the home of Mary and Martha, and while Martha prepared dinner, Mary sat at Jesus' feet and listened to Him. Martha was a little irritated. She was doing all the work and, perhaps, after she had forgotten to stir something on the stove, she finally lost it: "Lord, doesn't it seem unfair to you that my sister just sits here while I do all the work? Tell her to come and help me." What is just and fair appeals to the heart of God. Everything will be fair in eternity. Jesus could have said, *"Well, we've had a nice time now, Mary, but you really should go and help your sister."* If Jesus had said that, this story might have become the most famous Bible story in the world. Every Sunday School child would know this story better than the story of Jonah and the whale or Daniel in the lion's den! Every young believer would be taught that he or she must help with the chores. Parents would vote this as the most important teaching for their child!

However, the Lord had no such admonition for Mary. Getting the chores done was not His priority. A higher, more important reality was honored far above any sense of duty or even what was fair. He said:

> "My dear Martha, you are so upset over all these details. There is really only one thing worth being concerned about. Mary has discovered it – and I won't take it away from her." These quotes are from the NLT but the KJV says, "Martha, Martha, thou art careful and troubled about many things, but one thing is needful and Mary hath chosen that good part, which shall not be taken away from her."

ONE THING IS NEEDFUL! These are powerful words. I wish the story finished with something like this: *"So Martha dropped her spoon and fell to the Lord's feet and began worshipping and listening to the Lord also. Then the three of them had a wondrous time of sweet fellowship."* However, that probably did not happen; we can only suppose that Martha said a "harrumph" in her heart and kept right on going, stirring harder and rattling dishes. She lost out – big time.

"One thing is needful". Amazing! Say it again and again until your spirit really hears it. Our Savior, the Lord we love and serve, spoke these precious words. Does He really mean that? Don't we have to get our stuff done? Of course we do, but **one thing** is ABSOLUTELY NECESSARY. If the floor is not swept, the lawn is not mowed or the email is not answered, life will go on. But if we fail to sit and listen at Jesus' feet, life will not go on. But one may say, "What? I didn't sit at Jesus' feet yesterday and life still went on today". As a matter of fact someone may have never sat at Jesus feet just to listen and be in His presence, and yet life goes on daily year after year. But, the question must be asked—- what life? One thing is needful for the life the Lord calls us to here on the earth, and one thing is needful for eternity – Relationship.

A severe religious addiction in the American church is the need to get our doctrine straight. I have studied the Bible assiduously for over forty years, wanting to *get it right.* Knowledge is a big draw for many Americans. We want to know. In fact, most non-mainstream teachings from the Bible are based on the appeal of esoteric knowledge or "knowing more". Many Christians will quickly join a Bible Study before attending a prayer meeting, as learning and thinking may be easier than pouring our hearts out to God. However, the prayer meeting is apparently more necessary for our souls as Jesus stated: "one thing is needful". And the one thing was sitting at His feet, worshipping and listening.

We must honestly ask in light of Church History, just how important is having perfect doctrine to the Lord? He has been running His church, a church that was promised that the Gates of Hell would never prevail against it, for 2,000 years; and for over 75% of that time He ran it without Bibles! If having our doctrine just right is so critically important to the Lord, why didn't He give the printing press to the Romans? They were brilliant people with technology far ahead of their time. Some historians have reported that the Romans were working with a movable type system. But the Lord did not give that technology to man at that time. His people actually thrived on fragments of handwritten scrolls and, more importantly, they thrived on Relationship.

The Lord could have given His people Bibles and avoided what we call the "Dark Ages". But the Dark Ages only look dark to us; God has been walking through history in the Body of His Son, the Church, for 2,000 years and the Gates of Hell have never prevailed. We look at the lack of information and call it dark, but the Lord has always been looking for Relationship, over and above knowledge. No Gates of Hell have ever prevailed against Relationship. God's people have found real and vital Relationship while in prisons, in death camps, behind iron curtains, in total isolation, in torture, in underground churches, and mental institutions – all places where no Bibles were allowed. The Gates of Hell have never prevailed because Relationship is always possible. It is a lovely fact of history that the third verse of the famous hymn, *The Love of God,* was found scrawled on the wall of a mental institution:

> Could we with ink the ocean fill,
> And were the skies of parchment made,
> Were every stalk on earth a quill,
> And every man a scribe by trade,
> To write the love of God above,

Would drain the ocean dry.
Nor could the scroll contain the whole,
Though stretched from sky to sky.

It is said that these glorious words were found after the man had died. He was probably more sane than anyone in the asylum, or out on the streets for that matter. He was in a place where there was no Religion to interfere with or defile the awesome wonder of Relationship. In some ways, he is to be envied. If the beguiling and deceptive harlot, Religion, was not constantly seducing us away from our Beloved, what sweet freedom we would have. Our brother's life, deemed to be insane, may intimate to us that we might seem a little crazy if Relationship with God consumes us. Because the world is comfortable with Religion and uncomfortable with Relationship, we might be called insane, like our brother who perished in a cold, lonely asylum in the year 1050.

RELATIONSHIP – IT'S A COMMANDMENT

Lawyers are trained to be skilled both with words and with questions. The lawyers in Jesus' day often attempted to trip Him up with hard or ambiguous questions. These lawyers, who meticulously studied, dissected and analyzed the writings of the Law, often tried to corner the lowly Savior, but they were no match for His wisdom. Matthew 22:35-40 tells of one such occasion when a lawyer came to Jesus with a question "wanting to test Him", the Scripture says. "Master, which is the greatest commandment in the Law?" Without hesitation, Jesus referred to a verse in Deuteronomy and overlooked the Ten Commandments which had been written on tables of stone by God Himself. "Thou shalt love the Lord thy God with all thy heart, and with all thy soul, and with all thy mind." Even though the crafty lawyer only asked for one commandment, Jesus had to add a second one as He knew they were (and are) so closely related: "And the second is like it. Love your neighbor as yourself."

Concluding His answer, Jesus made an astonishing statement: "The entire law and all the demands of the prophets are based on these two commandments". Amazing! Just these two commandments fulfill everything ever taught, preached and written in Genesis, Exodus, Leviticus, Deuteronomy, Isaiah, Jeremiah, Ezekiel, Daniel, Hosea, Joel, Amos, Obadiah, Jonah, Micah, Nahum, Habakkuk, Zephaniah, Haggai, Zechariah and Malachi!! Hundreds of chapters and tens of thousands of words can all be thrown into a giant funnel and poured into just two commandments. So grand are these two commandments that they contain all instruction, wisdom, admonition, revelation, guidance, and truth of all the Law and the Prophets. Everything fits into loving God with all our hearts, souls and minds and loving others – because for God, it's all about Relationship.

Can there be any doubt about the Lord's ultimate goal and calling? He declares that Relationship is the Holy Key to fulfilling all that He has said to mankind. Perhaps we strain at doctrinal gnats and swallow the camel when our larger focus is learning and doing church activities instead of building a strong Relationship with God. It is true that one of the ways we love the Lord with our minds is by studying His Word and walking in the truths of Scripture; however, loving the Lord through the knowledge of His Word and faithfulness to the teachings of Scripture is only one part of loving Him. We must love Him completely with our hearts and our souls.

American culture is very fond of knowledge. We esteem knowledgeable people. We often feel safer in our minds than we do our hearts. Bible Studies are well attended, and yet the prayer meeting is almost in the museum of Church History. I have actually heard more than one person describe prayer as merely thinking about God and thinking about his or her requests. They have described how they "prayed all day" about a certain need because it was on their minds all day. Even if I were to think about someone all day, that focused thinking is *not relationship* until I pick up the phone or drive to his or her house and speak to that person directly. The Lord has called us to more than merely thinking about Him in our minds or giving Him our best thoughts. He wants to be spoken to directly with all our heart. Many people may feel safer in their minds because of painful events that have broken or injured their hearts, however, there is one COMPLETELY safe place for our hearts – with the Lord.

Chapter 5

BUILDING A CLOSE RELATIONSHIP

When the little shepherd boy, David, killed the nine-foot tall giant, Goliath, he picked up five smooth stones as his ammunition. He chose them carefully from a nearby stream and placed them in his shepherd's bag. He had only his shepherd's staff, a sling, and five rocks to go against the biggest and most heavily armed monster the Philistines could find. When he got close and heard the obnoxious taunts of the big bully, he pulled out a stone from his bag, whipped it around in his sling and, BAM, the stone found its target in the middle of Goliath's forehead. Wow, what a story. All he had was five smooth stones, but of course, he had much more than that. He had a Relationship with God.

The following list contains eight smooth stones chosen very carefully to bring the looming giant of Religion down. They kill the giant by cultivating a strong Relationship with the Lord. There were many other stones in the creek that day when David picked up his five, and there are other stones than these. But these are tested stones, their shapes are familiar to me and they are smooth stones, worn by use and time.

SMOOTH STONE #1–TIME

Americans love "how to" lessons and "how to" books. We want someone to explain how something works so we can just get it done. Unfortunately, the answer to the "how to" have a close relationship with the Lord is often an unwelcome answer:TIME. Your precious and fleeting time. Your seemingly never enough time. No shortcuts. No drive thru happy meals.

Life consists of this one element – TIME. Millions of people let the bulk of their entire lives be dictated to by a series of pressing obligations where their time never seems to be their own. The deception is that we can't take control of our time. However, in order to have a close relationship with the Lord we *must* take control of our time. Looking for a little leftover time will never do. We must take charge of our time and with determined purpose, give dedicated time to our Relationship with God.

Suppose Sam wants to form a meaningful relationship with Julie. He even hopes to marry her someday. How would he go about forming an intimacy with her? Would he begin to talk to all her friends and find out all about her? Would he collect pictures of her? Would he drive by and wave to her as she drove off work every day? If Sam is serious, none of these efforts would satisfy him. He must be WITH her. He must spend as much time as he can alone with her, sharing, laughing, telling stories, and listening to her. The parallel is obvious. It is no different with our Relationship with the Lord. Going to all Julie's friends and hearing about her is like listening to others – going to Bible studies, church services, seminars, conferences and reading books, all of which will NEVER be a substitute for personal time with the Lord. Driving by and waving will never do for Sam and praying on the run and talking to God while driving or doing chores will never do either.

Almost every American repeatedly declares "I just don't have enough time". But new things regularly come into our lives that require time and somehow we make time. Email, Facebook, a new dog, a new friend, a hobby all take some "extra" time we previously said we didn't have. However, if we want to keep in touch with friends and family, we make time for them. We make time for training and playing with the new puppy, and we make time to learn the new hobby. In other words, *we make time for what we really want to do.* If we truly desire a deeper relationship with God we will not look for time – we will make time for that Relationship.

SMOOTH STONE # 2 – THE PERSONHOOD OF GOD

Because our western culture is so cerebral we may forget the most basic of truths: God is a Person. This seems obvious, but often in our knowledge-based approach we lose sight of this very fundamental truth. We spend untold hours gaining knowledge *about* God, but less time *knowing* God.

Sally is a person; Steve is a person; Jason is a person; Carolyn is a person and on it goes. No two individuals are exactly alike. Each person has a unique DNA map as well as a unique history, distinctive ways, habits, thought patterns, ideas, values and goals. Each person is unique and different from any other person on earth. Above all the billions of unique individuals is the great Individual of all – God. He has His own ways, His own thought patterns, and values and goals that are distinctly His. Because God is a Person, He has a heart that can be blessed and given joy and a heart we can hurt and disappoint.

The syrupy, drippy, super religious love of God that is often preached today takes away from the Personhood of God and therefore leads away from Relationship. This false teaching projects the Lord like a radio station that emits a constant signal, 24 hours a day. This continuous, monotone or mono-emotion God is portrayed with statements like, "No matter what you do or say, the Lord loves you just the same" and "you cannot make Him love you any more or any less". How horrible! What a travesty and gross injustice to the Personhood of God.

It is true that God has a certain merciful, saving love that is reaching out to all of humanity because of the sacrifice of the Lord Jesus Christ. It is a constant flow of loving mercy for all people at all times. But God is a Person. When He is in Relationship with someone, the nature of His love changes. Once we are adopted by God into sonship through the new birth we are invited into *relational love,* and this love is altogether different from His merciful love. It is much like the parental love we are familiar with; we still love our children when they are disobedient or destructive, but a certain level of relationship and communication will be broken. Children, especially adult children, may so deeply violate the standards and values of the parents that relational love is severed almost completely while merciful and a longing to rescue love still exists. If we are living in sin and rebellion we have merciful love extended to us daily. However, the Lord makes it clear that He is in relational love only with those who love and obey Him. Jesus made this apparent in the following verses from John 14 and 15:

> **14:21** "Those who accept my commandments and obey them are the ones who love me. And because they love me, my Father will love them. And I will love them and reveal myself to each of them."
> **15:9** "I have loved you even as the Father has loved me. Remain in my love. **10** When you obey my commandments, you remain

> in my love, just as I obey my Father's commandments and remain in his love".
> **15:14** "You are my friends if you do what I command".

The first verse reveals that for this deeper, relational love to occur we must love the Son of God and because we love Him the Father will love us. The meaning is clear. Those who do not love the Son of God are not loved by God, at least not in the relational way that Jesus is depicting.

The second verse reveals that we do not always remain in that relational love; it is only when we obey Him. Jesus uses Himself as an example, telling us how He remained in His Father's love. It was through obedience.

The third verse gives us the one condition for being called a friend of God: obedience to His commands. James 4:4 also tells us that it is possible through disobedience to actually become the enemy of God:

> "You adulterers! Don't you realize that friendship with the world makes you an enemy of God? I say it again: If you want to be a friend of the world you make yourself an enemy of God."

Some may try to dismiss this verse as a warning to unbelievers, but the Book of James reveals in the first verses that it is written to believers. This completely dismisses the syrupy, religious teaching that He loves us all the time, just the same, no matter what.

These are strong words from the Book of James, but it is the Lord's goodness and His love that lets us know that it is entirely possible to become the enemy of God even as we remain in a position as a believer. This does not mean that He does not continue to have merciful love for us, but His approach and His attitude toward us will change. Because of His heart of love, His relationship with us will, for the most part, be centered around a call to repent and return to Him. Two verses later James calls the wandering sheep who have left the green pastures of relational love to enter into sorrow and deep grief:

> **7** So humble yourselves before God. Resist the devil, and he will flee from you. **8** Come close to God, and God will come close to you. Wash your hands, you sinners; purify your hearts, for your loyalty is divided between God

> and the world. **9** Let there be tears for what you have done. Let there be sorrow and deep grief. Let there be sadness instead of laughter, and gloom instead of joy. **10** Humble yourselves before the Lord, and he will lift you up in honor.

Both the emotion behind calling us enemies of God when we are too friendly with the world, and the emotion in this call to tears and deep grief, reveal the fervent emotions in God's heart.

The Lord also has very strong words from I John chapter 2 about the love we forfeit when we love the world.

> **15** Do not love this world nor the things it offers you, for when you love the world, you do not have the love of the Father in you.

By any interpretation, this reflects conditional love. God is a Person. He is not a robot-like entity that emits love 24/7 like a beam from a big tower. He feels our pain; He feels our sorrow; He is disappointed and offended by our disobedience; and He is blessed and engaged by our obedience.

Other verses in the New Testament also reveal the conditional nature of the love between God and His people. I John chapter two states:

> **4**. If someone claims, "I know God," but doesn't obey God's commandments, that person is a liar and is not living in the truth.
> **5.** But those who obey God's word truly show how completely they love him. That is how we know we are living in him.

Perhaps no other book in the Bible reveals the Personhood of God quite like Jeremiah. In this magnificent book, we are given insight into the heart of God as He expresses a myriad of emotions from anguish to zealous love and everything in between. Jeremiah is called "the weeping prophet" and yet, as we read the Book, we realize that he is crying the very tears of God. The Person of God comes alive through the prophet as he allows the reader to peer into the conflicted heart of the Lord. His conflict is the conflict of every parent: the need to punish and the pain of doing so to the one you love. God gave His people hundreds of years of mercy, beckoning and calling as he sent prophets, judges, kings and leaders to urge His people to turn back to Him. When Jeremiah ministered, it was at the end when the Lord knew He must punish His people for their rebellion and sin. One verse seems especially poignant:

> "Oh, Jerusalem, you are my beautiful and delicate daughter —but I will destroy you." Jer. 6:2

There it is – the heartbeat of God: He loves His people, yet He must make the choice sometimes to take us through the valley of the shadow of death to bring us to a place of submission and brokenness. We are His beautiful and delicate children, yet the sin lurking in our human nature must be destroyed, and it will hurt.

Lest we continue to fall for the drippy, radio tower style impersonal love, we should meditate on these verses from Hebrews chapter 12. These wonderful words beautifully reveal the parenting heart of the Father:

> **5** "My child, don't make light of the LORD's discipline, and don't give up when he corrects you. **6**
> For the LORD disciplines those he loves, and he punishes each one he accepts as his child." **7** As

> you endure this divine discipline, remember that God is treating you as his own children. Who ever heard of a child who is never disciplined by its father? **8** If God doesn't discipline you as he does all of his children, it means that you are illegitimate and are not really his children at all. **9** Since we respected our earthly fathers who disciplined us, shouldn't we submit even more to the discipline of the Father of our spirits and live forever? **10** For our earthly fathers disciplined us for a few years, doing the best they knew how. But God's discipline is always good for us, so that we might share in his holiness. **11** No discipline is enjoyable while it is happening—it's painful! But afterward there will be a peaceful harvest of right living for those who are trained in this way.

Being disciplined by the Lord is a very real part of His love. As the verses depict, we cannot be his children if we are without His hand of reprimand, which is painful (v. 11). This clear teaching also contradicts the mono-emotion God who acts and feels the same toward us all the time. Sometimes God must allow painful circumstances to come into our lives to mature us and bring "the peaceful harvest of right living".

When we allow our hearts to fully meditate on, and be open to, the unique Personhood of God, we will find refreshing reality in our Relationship with Him.

SMOOTH STONE #3–GET REAL

Suppose I lived next door to you and we had a "relationship". The biggest part of our relationship revolved around me asking to borrow things because your garage had every possible garden, yard and building tool in the world. Because you were a nice and generous neighbor, you gladly lent me tools and even helped me a little with a few projects. We visited a little about kids and dogs and gardens, but conversations never went too deep. Then one day I walked into your house and sat down. With a deep, needy sigh, I said, "Can I share the depths of my heart with you?" Wow! I have just radically changed the dynamics of that relationship. It will never be the same. If you believe that God is a Person, perhaps you can see how just asking for things will result in a very limited Relationship; we must get real with Him.

If you want to completely change the dynamics of your Relationship with God – GET REAL. Share the depths of your heart; tell Him your fears, doubts and the details of your thoughts. I have heard people say, "Well, He already knows how I feel anyway." Those who say things like that reveal that, to them, God is not a Person. Reading our thoughts is good enough for this intelligent but emotionless, blob called God. When a husband or wife communicates very little but simply depends on the other person's insight to read their thoughts and moods, that relationship is broken. All viable relationships require verbalizing the deepest thoughts of the heart. The most important Relationship, therefore, requires authentic communication.

Reading through the Psalms of David, the "man after God's own heart", it is apparent that David knew how to bare his soul. He tells the Lord about his anger, his fears, his sorrows and his ecstatic joys. David tells God how he wants to beat up on his enemies, and he tells God how tired he is of waiting for Him to act. Not everything David says is right or good, but it is real.

The Book of Ecclesiastes is a strange book in the Canon of Scripture. It is the record of the meditations and rantings of the heart of a depressed and backslidden man, Solomon. It is full of statements that aren't even true. Consider the opening verses of the Book:

> **2** "Everything is meaningless," says the Teacher, "completely meaningless!" **3** What do people get for all their hard work under the sun? **4** Generations come and generations go, but the earth never changes. **5** The sun rises and the sun sets, then hurries around to rise again. **6** The wind blows south, and then turns north. Around and around it goes, blowing in circles. **7** Rivers run into the sea, but the sea is never full. Then the water returns again to the rivers and flows out again to the sea. **8** Everything is wearisome beyond description. No matter how much we see, we are never satisfied. No matter how much we hear, we are not content.

The opening verse is simply not true. Everything is not meaningless; to the contrary, life is so meaningful that what we do counts for eternity! Why is a depressed and ranting king allowed on the platform of Scripture? For many reasons we can be sure. One reason surely is to show us just how meaningless life is without the Lord. King Solomon was quite probably the wealthiest man in the history of the world and very famous and powerful. However, without the Lord it was all vanity, or meaningless. The Book may also be important because of its value in seeing a heart get real. Solomon pours out his discouragement, his weariness with accomplishment, and the endless bondage of acquiring things. After pouring out his disillusionment for eleven chapters he is able to return to the Lord. The Book ends with this glorious conclusion:

> **13** That's the whole story. Here now is my final conclusion: Fear God and obey his commands, for this is everyone's duty. **14** God will judge us for everything we do, including every secret thing, whether good or bad. (Eccl. 12:13,14)

After twelve chapters of "spilling his guts" he finally got to the place of restoration. He realized his true place of rest: fear and obey

God. He overturns his repeated cry of all is meaningless by stating that we will all stand before the Lord and give an account for what we have done here on the earth.

Take heart from the Book of Ecclesiastes. Perhaps you are like Solomon sensing the vanity of acquiring things and working hard to maintain a certain pace of life. Tell the Lord all about it. We are so pushed along by life we are often completely out of touch with our own hearts. We are less than honest about our weariness or disappointments or heartaches because we spend little or no time in quiet meditation and communication with God. As we spend time in His presence we will know Him more but we will also understand ourselves more. Solomon's rambling and ranting words should encourage us to get real with God.

Peter was a man who all Christians appreciate. Unfortunately, it seems that often too much attention is given to Peter's mistakes. I have heard teaching that depicts Peter as the impulsive guy who always put his foot in his mouth. However, Jesus seemed to have an extraordinary bond with Peter. What contributed to the closeness Peter had with the Lord? Peter was for real. He said and did what others thought and wanted to do, but held back because of fear. Peter was not afraid to be real about how he felt, and his openness seemed to wonderfully engage the heart of the Lord.

In Matthew 16, Peter shows that his willingness to verbalize what he was thinking both took him down and lifted him up. Jesus turned to the disciples one day and said, "Who do men say that I am?" They all began to chime in telling what they had heard. They were telling Jesus how some said he was John the Baptist and then again there were rumors that he was Elijah or Jeremiah. Then the Lord put the question directly to them: "But who do you say that I am?". This time He was met with silence – except from Peter. "You are the Christ, the Son of the Living God", Peter blurts out. Jesus' response must have made all the others think, "Wow I wish I had said that".

> **17** Jesus replied**,** "You are blessed, Simon son of John, because my Father in heaven has revealed this to you. You did not learn this from any human being.
> **18** Now I say to you that you are Peter (which means 'rock'), and upon this rock I will build my church, and all the powers of hell will not conquer it."

Peter's profession of the true identity of the Lord revealed by the Spirit would be the very foundation of the church. Millions of people believe in the Lord's identity as the Son of God but they have simply learned it as a fact, or "learned it from a human being" as Jesus said. But something about the way Peter said it let the Lord know that Peter had received the truth directly from God; it had been revealed to him. This spiritual understanding is so profound it forms a foundation in our souls that cannot be shaken even by the powers of hell.

Peter was honored and commended by Christ for his confession. In the very next passage in Matthew 16 Peter again bares his soul. Jesus told the disciples that He must go to Jerusalem and suffer at the hands of the religious elders and be killed. Perhaps all the others felt as strongly as Peter, but Peter was the only one to verbalize his abhorrence at the thought of Jesus suffering and dying. The Scripture tell us that Peter actually began to rebuke, or reprimand the Lord:

> **22** But Peter took him aside and began to reprimand him for saying such things. "Heaven forbid, Lord," he said. "This will never happen to you!"

> **23** Jesus turned to Peter and said, "Get away from me, Satan! You are a dangerous trap to me. You are seeing things merely from a human point of view, not from God's."

Peter was so real. It cost him serious rebuke, to the point of being called Satan; but his ability to be real and say what was on his heart brought him blessings as well and made him a much loved disciple. His clarity and honesty opened the way for a vital Relationship with the Lord.

Just six days later, Peter was privileged to be among the three disciples that were taken up a mountain where they saw the Lord transfigured with blazing light. Moses and Elijah suddenly appeared and were speaking with Him. The whole experience was totally supernatural. Peter, beside himself with excitement, blurted out his foolish idea about building three tabernacles on the mountain for Jesus, Moses and Elijah. The Scripture says that while Peter was still speaking, the voice of God thundered and said, "This is my beloved Son, listen to Him". (Matt. 17:5) Apparently, God was responding to Peter's zealous cry of building the three tabernacles. It was as if God was saying, "The only One who counts here is My Son." Later as Peter wrote his epistles he was able to say:

> **16** ...We saw his majestic splendor with our own eyes **17** when he received honor and glory from God the Father. The voice from the majestic glory of God said to him, "This is my dearly loved Son, who brings me great joy."**18** We ourselves heard that voice from heaven when we were with him on the holy mountain. (2 Pet. 1: 16-18)

Regardless of how readers of the Scripture look at Peter – bumbling, too talkative, bold, or rash – he was **real** about what he was thinking and feeling. The Lord never had to read his thoughts; he said it all. We can learn from our brother, Peter. What we want to say may not be right, true, or spiritual but if it's real – that is, if it's what is really in our hearts, we need to share it with the Lord. We need to be totally open with Him and tell Him everything, including our doubts or anger or our inability to forgive. It all fits on His Fatherly shoulders. The Lord can handle it, and it brings us into a place of closeness that we can't have any other way. Being real with the Lord also builds our Relationship so that He is more real with us. He can show us things and speak to our hearts with a new liberty because we have been open and honest with Him.

SMOOTH STONE #4–CONFESSION AND REPENTANCE

A healthy and real relationship with the Lord will include repentance; it will be an ongoing and integral part of close fellowship with God. Repentance is one of the very sweetest moments between our hearts and God's heart. A time of contrition in the Lord's Presence is a special treasure, a cherished and holy moment like none else. It is a piece of eternity when time seems to stand still and it is you and the Lord alone in the universe. We must take off our shoes. The ground is holy. We are blessed beyond measure as we sense our weakness, helplessness and nakedness. We become wonderfully vulnerable as we open our souls to His touch. Our Heavenly Father responds with tender love when we come as erring and repentant children, in a way that is like none other.

That level of vulnerability is something we hide from. It is a rare event on this earth to be so weak and open in front of another person, for we know how deeply we could be injured. But our Father has a sweet and wonderful response to all who are willing to come naked and bare their souls; we never need to hide from Him.

Repentance is one of the most overlooked blessings in our lives. Sincere followers of the Lord may tell a Christian friend something like, "I got so convicted today when I said a sharp word to someone." And indeed, he or she should have been convicted and undoubtedly sensed the Lord's displeasure. However, where that person might have missed the blessing was not taking it into the Lord's Presence and letting God really deal with the root, perhaps impatience or buried anger. Being convicted by the Holy Spirit is an invitation to enter in to the holy ground of sweet repentance; it is God's beckoning to come closer and meet with Him, in Spirit and in truth.

Repentance is a gift; it is by invitation only. We cannot conjure or work up that sense of total nakedness and vulnerability. We can't simply decide to have a broken and contrite heart before God. It must be led and orchestrated by the Holy Spirit. We certainly are able to come to the Lord in humble confession of our irritability, anger, lust, love of the world etc. And He is ready to take us into authentic repentance, but often *we* are not ready. We only want to be forgiven for the leaves on the tree. We are not ready to have Him deal with the trunk and the roots. That level of repentance takes us to the place of total nakedness and exposure, and we may not be willing to go there. But be sure of this: *To stay away from that place of total vulnerable repentance is to stay away from the heart of God.* We may think the price is too high to enter into that deep level of contrition. We will have to be totally honest about ourselves in a way that makes us uncomfortable. However, the price is much higher for **not** going to that place of repentance for we forfeit closeness with God. No price is higher than that.

One of the most beautiful chapters in the Bible has to be Psalm 51. King David pours out his heart in full repentance in this Psalm. It was written after he was confronted by Nathan the prophet about his adultery with Bathsheba and the plot that killed her husband. There is much to learn from this Psalm about real repentance. Consider the first four verses:

> **1** Have mercy on me, O God, because of your unfailing love. Because of your great compassion,

> blot out the stain of my sins. **2** Wash me clean from my guilt. Purify me from my sin. **3** For I recognize my rebellion; it haunts me day and night. **4** Against you, and you alone, have I sinned; I have done what is evil in your sight. You will be proved right in what you say, and your judgment against me is just.

David never discusses any of the particulars about the sins he committed; his grave concern is for the ugly stain of sin on his soul. He senses the defiling nature of sin and, as he stated, it haunted him. The true purity of his repentance is revealed in verse four: "Against you, and you alone, have I sinned..." Some readers may want to disagree with David; he sinned against Bathsheba, her husband Uriah, and all Uriah's family who lost a son, a brother, an uncle or a friend. However, David's prayer resonates with pure and authentic remorse. Above all, our sin is against God.

It may be hard to grasp that if we speak an unkind word, or act arrogantly toward someone, that we have sinned against God. However, we have indeed hurt His heart and offended Him. Seeing this reality, which can only be revealed by the Holy Spirit, will lead to both a cleansing and a release that our sin-scarred souls crave.

We may also be tempted to think that since we have not committed the "really bad sins" like David did, we don't need such all-consuming and broken repentance. But all sin is sin. It is all heinous; and all of it, including our petty pride and unkind thoughts, cost God the life of His dear Son. By qualifying sin, we are expressing that somehow our sin is cleaner or prettier than David's. That type of thinking in itself is arrogant and should drive us to our knees in humility earnestly seeking cleansing. If we ever allow the Holy Spirit to show us the vile and detestable nature of our sin, it will drive us into the arms of our Heavenly Father like nothing else. For He alone has the remedy for shame and guilt.

In the next five verses David continues to cry for relief from the deep sense of sin and a broken relationship.

> **7** Purify me from my sins, and I
> will be clean; wash me, and I will
> be whiter than snow. **8** Oh, give
> me back my joy again; you have
> broken me— now let me rejoice.
> **9** Don't keep looking at my sins.
> Remove the stain of my guilt. **10**

> Create in me a clean heart, O God. Renew a loyal spirit within me. **11** Do not banish me from your presence, and don't take your Holy Spirit from me.

David's cries might seem repetitive or redundant, but this model prayer is showing us that we should spend time and be thorough with God when we have come into the holy Throne Room of sorrow for our sin. Many may want a quick and easy form of repentance and call out a quick, "forgive me, God" prayer and get on with life. It is true that the Lord is quick to forgive and we need not repeat ourselves over and over to get His forgiveness. However, repentance is a sacred and solemn event between our hearts and God's heart. In that eternal moment, time is irrelevant. We should stay in His Presence and wait upon Him to do the entire work. The open door of our hearts through humility and brokenness provides an important time for His hand to do a profound and lasting work. In David's words in the same psalm:

> **17** The sacrifice you desire is a broken spirit. You will not reject a broken and repentant heart, O God.

Confession and repentance should be an ongoing and lovely part of a genuine Relationship with God. If it has been a while since the sweetness of this honest and vulnerable time has occurred between you and your Lord, ask Him to send His Holy Spirit to draw you into His presence in a powerful way the next time you need forgiveness. Spend time with that stone until it is a well-worn smooth stone, ready to take down the giant.

SMOOTH STONE #5 – PERSEVERANCE AND PATIENCE

Just in case this fact has escaped notice let it be stated with clarity: God is never in a hurry.

I had a very good friend once who was an old rancher. I loved to visit with him about ranching and the good 'ol days. As I watched him over the years I observed that he never was in a hurry. I would tear into the driveway at his ranch, out of breath, explaining that I needed to borrow his truck because my car had broken down. He never moved any faster no matter how much pressure I exerted. My brother and I joked about him one day calling him "Mr. One Gear" and laughingly saying that his one gear was compound low. He was extremely pleasant to be around, and I think it was because of his patient attitude toward life. I think God is Mr. One Gear – and it's compound low.

The Lord doesn't appear to respond to my pressure or my "I want it now" prayer antics. To the contrary, what He seems to respond to is patient, serious, consistent, perseverance —- YUK! Those words make my flesh crawl. My human nature cries out for instant gratification. Patiently waiting on God has no appeal to me.

We have two teaching parables in the Bible about prayer. They are both recorded in Luke and both teach the same lesson about prayer: it must be persevering. The parable in Luke 11 was discussed in the section about seeking God with an undivided heart. But we must look at it a little deeper. It is the Lord's direct teaching about prayer and the power of perseverance. Before Jesus gives His illustration, the disciples specifically ask Him to teach them to pray. He first gives them a model for prayer we call The Lord's Prayer, and then He tells a parable to further instruct them:

> **5** Then, teaching them more about prayer, he used this story: "Suppose you went to a friend's house at midnight, wanting to

> borrow three loaves of bread.
> You say to him, **6** 'A friend of
> mine has just arrived for a visit,
> and I have nothing for him to
> eat.' **7** And suppose he calls out
> from his bedroom, 'Don't bother
> me. The door is locked for the
> night, and my family and I are
> all in bed. I can't help you. **8** But
> I tell you this—though he won't
> do it for friendship's sake, if you
> keep knocking long enough, he
> will get up and give you what-
> ever you need because of your
> shameless persistence. **9** And so
> I tell you, keep on asking, and
> you will receive what you ask for.
> Keep on seeking, and you will
> find. Keep on knocking, and the
> door will be opened to you. **10**
> For everyone who asks, receives.
> Everyone who seeks, finds. And
> to everyone who knocks, the
> door will be opened."

This story makes most of us a little uncomfortable. Is Jesus likening God to a sleepy, reluctant friend? If we think so, we are misreading the parable, for it is only a story depicting the need for perseverance.

Through the parable the Lord is not teaching us about God, but rather He is answering the disciples' request to know more about prayer. The Lord's clear teaching is that the quality of prayer that catches His ear is sincere, consistent, and persevering.

Even Hollywood recognizes the stellar quality of perseverance. The Lone Ranger and Marshall Dillon persevere through Indian attacks, ambushes, river crossings and hours of tracking the outlaw, until finally they overcome. Joe has to persevere past the ridicule that he's too young to race and he pushes through all that hinders him. At last, he wins it all and the trophy is his. The Survivor must persevere; Secretariat, the racehorse, and the team must hold on through the losing streak to become the best in the world. And on and on it goes. We can't get enough of the perseverance story, and Hollywood can't use the story too many times. Admittedly, it makes for a great movie about other peoples' lives. We just don't want our own life script to read that way.

What is it that Hollywood sees that makes perseverance such a compelling theme? It's the same thing God sees: it brings out the best in us. The Luke 11 story is not about a reluctant God, but a Parenting God who is beckoning us to become a person of strong character. It's about a Loving God who wants to bring out the best in us and guide us into Relationship. It's about a Teaching God who wants us to develop the strong spiritual muscle of never-give-up faith.

There are other signal reasons why the Lord wants us to learn perseverance. God is all about Relationship. It is everything to Him. He wants a profound and sincere relationship with His people, not a trivial *ask and get the stuff you want* relationship. If the Lord granted every wish when we asked, we would simply relate to Him as the Big Sugar Daddy in the sky. He beckons us to ask, seek and knock, but our goals are often different. He is seeking Relationship and we are seeking action, but in the course of our consistent seeking, we find the beauty and grandeur of His Presence and experience intimacy in our Relationship.

The other parable the Lord used to teach about prayer is found in Luke 18.

> **1** One day Jesus told his disciples a story to show that they should always pray and never give up.**2** "There was a judge in a certain city," he said, "who neither feared God nor cared about people. **3** A widow of that

> city came to him repeatedly, saying, 'Give me justice in this dispute with my enemy'. **4** The judge ignored her for a while, but finally he said to himself,' I don't fear God or care about people, **5** but this woman is driving me crazy. I'm going to see that she gets justice, because she is wearing me out with her constant requests!'" **6** Then the Lord said, "Learn a lesson from this unjust judge. **7** Even he rendered a just decision in the end. So don't you think God will surely give justice to his chosen people who cry out to him day and night? Will he keep putting them off? **8** I tell you, he will grant justice to them quickly! But when the Son of Man returns, how many will he find on the earth who have faith?"

There it is again—persistence and perseverance. God will give justice to those "who cry out to Him day and night." Jesus calls the judge an unjust man; however, He uses him to teach us something: He says, "Learn a lesson from this unjust judge." What should we learn from this hard-hearted unrighteous man? That *even he* will respond to someone who never gives up – so how much more will our Righteous God hear the cries of His persevering child?

Some students of Scripture may find Jesus' teachings from Matthew Chapter 6 to be a contradiction to the parables about perseverance:

> **7** "When you pray, don't babble on and on as people of other religions do. They think their prayers are answered merely by repeating their words again and again. **8** Don't be like them, for your Father knows exactly what you need even before you ask him!"

Crying out to the Lord "day and night" is honored in the parable, but seemingly warned against in these words.

This NLT translation provides some clarity that is not readily available in the traditional King James wording which states "they think they will be heard for their much speaking". The teaching is not about the persevering child of God who petitions God repeatedly for his or her need.

Rather, the admonition is not to use "vain repetitions" or "repeating words again and again". It is about memorized phrases or words that are said almost like a repetitious mantra in the Hindu religion. Most heathen religions have special phrases to repeat or memorized prayers, and use instruments such as prayer wheels or beads to help the worshipper rehearse and recite the words. The verses from Matthew six, however, were taught to followers of Christ. Jesus knew that The Christian church also would be guilty of using repetitive phrases and prayers. Earnest and needy prayers may contain the same request without using monotonous words and repeated prayers.

If we are going to be in Relationship with God, or with anybody for that matter, we need to be sincere and speak words from our hearts. If we said the same words over and over and over again to our spouse, or a friend, after a while, it would become meaningless noise. The Personhood of God (Smooth Stone #2) requires that we speak from our hearts and share details with Him about our thoughts, hopes, needs, sorrows, heartaches and fears. All of it interests Him. If we think He is not interested in the nuts and bolts and small fragments of our lives, then we simply do not know Him very well.

SMOOTH STONE #6–SUFFERING

Apostle Paul makes an amazing statement in Philippians 3:10 after telling us that he has counted everything in his life as refuse or garbage compared to the excellency of knowing the Lord.

> **8** Yes, everything else is worthless when compared with the infinite value of knowing Christ Jesus my Lord. For his sake I have discarded everything else, counting it all as garbage, so that I could gain Christ **9** and become one with him. I no longer count on my own righteousness through obeying the law; rather, I become righteous through faith in Christ. For God's way of making us right with himself depends on faith. **10** I want to know Christ and experience the mighty power that raised him from the dead. I want to suffer with him, sharing in his death.

What was that last part, Paul? We were all with you, saying a hearty, Yes and Amen until that last part. You want to *suffer* with Him??

And share in His death?? Perhaps you have had too much time out in the Arabian Desert in the hot sun, Paul. (Galatians 1:17,18)

In reality, Paul is handing us a smooth stone out of his own shepherd's bag that will keep us near to God's heart. The KJV uses the beautiful phrase, "the fellowship of His sufferings, being made conformable to His death". Jesus is the Man of Sorrows, and God the Father has so anguished over His lost creation that He was willing to sacrifice His own Son. When we get near Him, we will be near suffering. If we are in rich fellowship with Him, we will be beckoned into the holy place of the fellowship of His sufferings.

Even the world understands the fellowship of suffering. Cancer survivors have a special bond; war veterans who suffered together have a lifelong connection; people who have endured loss of children get together and understand each other like no one else can. We have support groups for health crises, heartbreaks, grief, and loss because people find a special bond with each other when they suffer the same sorrow. The fellowship of suffering is so powerful, it provides more than understanding; it provides healing.

We are invited by God Himself to suffer with Him both by sharing His sorrow and sharing our sorrows. We suffer as we share His pain and sorrow over a lost and rebellious world and we suffer through the sorrows of this life. He beckons us to share every facet of our pain with Him. And that is the fork in the road for the whole world of sufferers. Will we let our pain drive us into His arms? Will we share every tear and every thought with Him and allow the beauty of the fellowship of suffering to heal us?

Millions of people look at the smooth stones in the creek bed of life and reject this stone. They do everything but fellowship with God in their sorrow. They spend all their energies questioning, saying it's not fair, rebuking the devil, and languishing in despair and self-pity. What a supreme tragedy, when the Man of Sorrows stands close by, waiting to give Himself to the suffering child in a way that is rich beyond compare.

Many earnest believers may say, "But I did pray over and over and God did nothing." Many miss HIM, though, because the only focus of their prayers is for God to fix their dilemma and stop the suffering. Sometimes God is not going to cure your beloved spouse, friend, or sister, but He is going to cure something in you and in the sufferer. He is going to offer you something *better* than a cure; He offers Himself in a very deep heart-to-heart way that can be experienced no other way.

In Matthew chapter five, Jesus gives us eight of His own smooth stones taken out of the Great Shepherd's heart. These are the precious gems of life called the Beatitudes – or the Blesseds. These smooth stones are the essence of happiness, a goal pursued by all people. The word "blessed" used here means supremely happy, even to the point of being envied by others for such intense happiness. The second stone, a key to immeasurable happiness, reads like this:

> **4** God blesses those who mourn,
> for they will be comforted.

We don't agree, Jesus. We think it should read, *"Blessed are they that mourn, for the Lord will remedy the situation for them."* But the Lord offers nothing about the source of our mourning; what He offers the mourning soul is His comfort. He offers the rewarding and effective healing virtue of fellowship in sufferings. Ask a sufferer who is leaving a meeting of parents who have lost children what he or she got out of the meeting? They may say something like "just some comfort and understanding". "What?" the inquirer might ask, "Is that all you got by driving across town to get to this meeting? In light of your great loss, was it worth it?" The answer will be "Yes".

Ask the sufferer who has walked through the valley of the shadow of death and has leaned hard on the Lord, if he or she received something precious and rich. If we receive special comfort and understanding by sharing in an earthly setting, how much more might we receive when we draw close and walk with the "God of all comfort". This is not to minimize the comfort we may receive from one another; it is God's plan for us to comfort one another with what we have received from Him. (2 Cor. 1:3-6) However, the comfort we receive directly from God brings us deeper into that personal one-on-one relationship like nothing else. The Lord Himself beckons each of His children to use this smooth stone. It is well-worn by many sufferers who have received the grand invitation to draw near to Him whose hands and side bear scars of suffering. The communion we are invited to share in our darkest hours is at the heart of who God is.

Unfortunately, we may miss the depths of His healing comfort because we want more. But the Lord understands this. He has heard our sorrowful cries for relief from the pain. He has compassion for, and gives comfort to all mourners, no matter what they say or how they cry unto Him. He is always there, and often He does deliver and bring healing or relief. However, when He chooses not to, He offers something of inestimable worth, exceedingly precious and valuable: communion and camaraderie with His own suffering Heart.

Perhaps the most beautiful Christian book ever written on the reality, meaning, and theology of suffering is by Joni Eareckson Tada and Steve Estes called, *When God Weeps*. Joni has a well-educated voice about suffering, only her education was not in the halls of academia, but rather the continual suffering of a quadriplegic living in a wheelchair. She makes a statement in that book that needs to be heard by God's people everywhere:

> "God's plan – not plan B or C or D, but *His plan* calls for Christians to suffer, sometimes intensely. God will write light moments into the script of our lives, but without fail, some scenes are going to break your heart, some of your favorite characters will die, and the movie may end earlier than you wish." (p. 56)

What are we going to do with this statement? Some may consider this the statement of a defeated Christian who didn't have enough faith to be healed. But Scripture does not back that position, and those kinds of statements make the work of God about *us* and not *Him*. To the contrary, Scripture backs up Joni's statement from Genesis to Revelation. If God did not *intend* for His servants to suffer then we must stand in awe of what a very poor job He has done in protecting His people. Abel, Abraham, Moses, Samuel, David, Jeremiah, Daniel, Ezekiel, Paul, Peter, John all really suffered. Indeed, the great Hall of Fame in chapter 11 of Hebrews ends with this triumphant statement about God's great men and women of faith:

> But others were tortured, refusing to turn from God in order to be set free. They placed their hope in a better life after the resurrection. **36** Some were jeered at, and their backs were cut open with whips. Others were chained in prisons. **37** Some died by stoning, some were sawed in half, and others were killed with the sword. Some went about wearing skins of sheep and goats, destitute and

> oppressed and mistreated. **38** They were too good for this world, wandering over deserts and mountains, hiding in caves and holes in the ground. **39** All these people earned a good reputation because of their faith, yet none of them received all that God had promised.

Verse 39 is perhaps quite disturbing for those who believe that faith will heal everything to their liking. The great saints who suffered so severely had faith and yet "none of them received all that God had promised." Why did God let all this suffering happen to his people? Because suffering is part of this life and suffering is part of God's life. We cannot be close to Him without meeting together in that valley. And God intends for us to find richness and beauty in the fellowship of suffering. Joni Eareckson says it this way:

> "Tears never tasted so good until I entered the fellowship of Christ's sufferings. Until then I never wept bitterly over lost souls and a hurting world. The ache in my heart never felt so fiery and passionate. Sorrow

> and joy never seemed so sweetly mingled. Hope never seemed so solid.... Affliction is the grist-mill where pride is reduced to powder, leaving our souls naked, bare, and bonded to Christ. And it feels beautiful" (p. 143)

The truth that seems to be lacking in much Christian teaching today is the *value* of suffering. Consider this verse from Romans chapter eight, such a doctrinally rich chapter in the New Testament:

> **17** And since we are his children, we are his heirs. In fact, together with Christ we are heirs of God's glory. But if we are to share his glory, we must also share his suffering.

Suffering not only has great value in our Relationship with the Lord, but also has important eternal worth. Apparently, the condition for sharing His glory in eternity, hinges on whether we are willing to first suffer with Him. For me, suffering took on a much deeper value when I was considering these verses about our glorious future recorded in Revelation chapter 21:

> **3** I heard a loud shout from the throne, saying, "Look, God's home is now among his people! He will live with them, and they will be his people. God himself will be with them. **4** He will wipe every tear from their eyes, and there will be no more death or sorrow or crying or pain. All these things are gone forever."

Someday, the beauty and richness of suffering with Him will be available no more. My redemption was purchased through suffering; my deliverance came through suffering; my healing came through suffering; my invitation to the Wedding Banquet of heaven was written in the blood of His suffering! Should I resist and kick and scratch and bite when my suffering comes and never know the fellowship He offered me? Once this life is over, that precious offer is no more.

SMOOTH STONE #7 - OBEDIENCE

I had a beautiful Labrador retriever who was a great hiking companion. I had also trained her to run alongside when I rode my bicycle. She was a great dog. One afternoon, someone told me about a Border collie at the local shelter who was going to be put down the next day, unless she was adopted. I said, "Well, I'll just go look." When I got there I was astounded at what a beautiful dog she was, and I brought her home. I immediately began calling friends trying to find her another home. I was sure I could find her a good home. However, weeks went by and still she was with me. I began to realize that this dog had the ultimate hook to rivet my heart to hers. It was impossible to resist. I felt guilty toward my other dog because this new dog was pulling my heart right out of my soul with a key my other dog didn't have —- the key of OBEDIENCE. Everything I told her to do she did, no hesitation. She stared at me waiting for permission to go, or instructions to stay. She hung on my every word, my every look, and my every movement, wanting to obey my wishes.

I walked out of my house one day after giving her just a simple motion to let her know she was not going; she simply submitted even though she wanted to go. I suddenly realized that obedience to me was more important to her than anything else. I went in the garage, got in my vehicle, and began weeping. "Lord, do I look at You like that? Do I hang on Your every word, wanting to only obey? Do I wait for Your word before I move? Is obedience to You more precious than having my own way?" That dog changed my life.

I realized as never before that I had a key to open the heart of God *to me* in a profound way. It was called obedience. I began to take cues from my dog and seek the Lord for His guidance at every turn. I waited for His word to my heart with only one goal in mind: to obey Him, and therefore please Him.

Any parent can confirm that obedience is a key to relationship. If a child is constantly testing the rules and disobeying when he perceives he might get away with it, the parent can't focus as much on relationship. That mother or father must be constantly working on bringing that child into compliance. The Lord's parenting work with us is similar. If we have disobedience in our lives, serving other gods such as work, earthly gain, lust, too much TV, pride, etc., then He must spend His energies with us bringing us into compliance. On the other hand, if we develop refined obedience, it opens the door for God to speak to us and guide us into a new adventurous life, led by His Spirit.

Moses, undoubtedly, is our best example in the Word of a man in Relationship with God. This is quite interesting since he is an Old Testament man, even God's lawgiver. However, we must remember that the New Covenant began with Abraham who entered into a profound relationship with God through faith 430 years before the Law was ever given. We are, therefore, called the children of Abraham. As taught in Galatians chapter three, the giving of the Law hundreds of years later did not cancel or mitigate the faith covenant, which we call the New Covenant. The door to a close relationship with God has always been open to all those who sought after it. Moses was not excluded from the Relationship we can enjoy, and there is nothing that excludes us from what Moses had with God.

> "Inside the Tent of Meeting, the Lord would speak to Moses face to face, as one speaks to a friend..." (Ex. 33:11)

In another passage, God is speaking to Moses' brother and sister who had criticized their brother, and God Himself says this about Moses:

> "If there were prophets among you, I, the Lord, would reveal myself in visions. I would speak to them in dreams. But not with my servant Moses. Of all my house he is the one I trust. I

> speak to him face to face, clearly and not in riddles! He sees the Lord as he is. So why were you not afraid to criticize my servant Moses?"(Numbers 12:6-8)

These are certainly amazing words spoken by God Himself. We were created for this level of Relationship and this passage should make our hearts hunger and thirst for such reality. The striking verse of this passage that says so much is, "of all My house, he is the one I trust". That is simply take-my-breath-away, astonishingly beautiful. I may spend my life learning to trust God, but perhaps I should spend my life being the person God can trust.

Once I settled into having two dogs, I worked hard at treating them equally. After all, my sweet Lab was a good dog. But it was all to no avail. The consistent, dedicated obedience of my Border Collie brought her into a privileged status because – *I could trust her.* She went everywhere with me and rarely had to stay home because she was obedient in any situation. I began to realize how crucial my obedience to God was. I was becoming a person He could trust, and I began hearing Him speak and lead me in a more detailed way than I had ever experienced in my life. He took me to new heights in prayer; He began to teach me with astounding insight when I opened His Word; and I had a new freedom and wisdom when ministering to others. Obedience to Him had become my priority. My faithful dog preached it to me every day; I could not avoid the reminder.

With more of His voice and more spiritual understanding came a new responsibility. One afternoon, I heard a mother say this statement to her child when she was telling her to do something: "Delayed obedience is no obedience at all". I wanted to drop to the floor and weep when I heard that. Suddenly I understood with extreme clarity something that the Lord was dealing with me about. **"Delayed obedience is no obedience at all"** kept ringing in my heart. I couldn't get away from it. I began to realize that I had very rudely said "Later" to God several times, and obeyed Him on my own terms, which was <u>no obedience at all</u>.

Can God trust us to obey immediately when He speaks? Perhaps we have ceased hearing regularly from God because we have not responded to instructions He has already given us. An important question for consideration in all aspects of our lives is: Can God trust us? Can we be trusted to wait on Him for guidance as to why He blessed us materially, for example? Perhaps it is to build an orphanage in India and not an addition on our house. Do we look to Him at every turn to hear His word before proceeding? Can He trust us with our gifts, abilities and talents to make sure they are used first for the Kingdom of God? That is not to say that if we can't be trusted and we spend all His blessings on ourselves He will make our lives miserable. It only means that Relationship will have some limitations, and Religion will fill the void.

Obedience is very difficult. We are self-willed to the core. A continuous life of obedience requires brokenness, humility and patience — things we do not have in our human nature. We may be a rather patient and giving person, but we are NOT without a strong will that resists being broken. Our will can be trained like the lion in the circus that can be taught to jump through the hoops. We can train ourselves to be religious, nice, and sweet and jump through the right hoops. Inside, however, lurks the untamed creature who wants things to go our way. We must learn to be obedient, and it comes through life's hardest lessons.

We may be surprised to learn that as Jesus walked among us as a Man, He also had to learn obedience. Hebrews 5:8 tells us:

> "Even though Jesus was God's Son, He learned obedience from the things He suffered."

We so wish it said something like, *"He learned obedience from the blessings of God"*. Because, if Jesus had to learn obedience by suffering, what hope do we have to learn it any other way? Apparently, smooth stone #6 and #7 belong in the same bag. While we learn to fellowship in His sufferings, we are also learning to walk in obedience.

We can never take obedience too seriously. The Lord equates obedience with love, as evidenced by these verses from the Gospel of John:

> **14:21** "Those who accept my commandments and obey them are the ones who love me. And because they love me, my Father will love them. And I will love them and reveal myself to each of them."

> **15:10** When you obey my commandments, you remain in my love, just as I obey my Father's commandments and remain in his love".

Somehow I missed the conditional nature of these verses and others until the Lord sent my dog to me. She was the most convicting preacher I ever sat under. So if you need a reminder to seek the Lord regularly for an obedient heart, go get a Border Collie.

SMOOTH STONE #8 — LOVING HIS LOST WORLD

If we are near the heart of God we will come to know His zealous and impassioned heartbeat for His lost children. Hurting, caring, and weeping for lost rebellious people is contrary to our nature. We will NEVER sense it without being close enough to hear and to feel His beating heart for the lost. In fact, Religion provides a great escape from the crucifying experience of sharing God's love for His lost sheep. We can give to missions, help with programs, support the youth mission team, and listen to stirring messages without ever having our hearts broken.

Getting close to the Lord where He can share His burden is costly. We may have to go to the grocery store and share with someone and risk our worldly reputation. We may have to go on a mission trip, or give money away to help the poor in India who live at the city dump, licking food containers. We may risk putting that burden into our children's hearts who may want to go live near that city dump in India. There are huge risks in carrying this smooth stone. Religion is much safer.

Consider the Lord's teachings in Luke 15:

> **4** "If a man has a hundred sheep and one of them gets lost, what will he do? Won't he leave the ninety-nine others in the wilderness and go to search for the one that is lost until he finds it?
> **5** And when he has found it, he will joyfully carry it home on his shoulders. **6** When he arrives, he will call together his friends and neighbors, saying, 'Rejoice with me because I have found my lost sheep.'**7** In the same way, there is more joy in heaven over one lost sinner who repents and returns to God than over ninety-nine others who are righteous and haven't strayed away!

I believe it is safe to extrapolate from this story that while we are huddled together on Sunday morning safely with the 99, the biggest part of the Lord's heart is outside the doors looking for the lost. But, looking for the lost with the Lord is not very safe. There are wolves out there and barbed wire and rivers to cross while searching for that lost sheep. It's much safer to hang out with the herd. The pain of rejection, mockery, and failure all await us if we care for lost sheep. Sending money to missionaries and letting them face adversity is so much easier. Nowhere in the Scripture are we told that reaching out to lost people is just for special people with a "calling". It's everyone's calling. However, we will never care enough to reach out and leave our comfort zone without coming in direct contact with God's heartbeat for this rebellious world.

What can possibly motivate us to leave our deeply rooted self-love behind and truly care for lost souls? If we read about the rich man in hell, burning with thirst, will his screams send us out? If we read adventurous and faith-filled stories about missionaries and soul winners, will that call us away from our selfish hearts? Should we attend a missions' convention to be stirred to hear His call? Perhaps all of these can contribute to a fresh love and commitment to lost souls, but one avenue is sure to get us there – get close, really close to God. Get close enough to weep with Him; close enough to rejoice with Him, and close enough to behold with our hearts, the cross.

When we draw near to God and spend time in His presence, we will find at the core of His Being is the Cross. The Cross is at the forefront of all that He is, and all He has to say. The depths of what happened there cannot be fathomed with our minds. "Christ died for our sin" and "God so loved the world He gave His only Son..." barely ripple the surface of a bottomless ocean. Only in the next life might we be able to plummet the depths of the cross of Christ.

In some ways, it is a shame that we wear pretty gold crosses as jewelry, and erect beautiful wooden crosses in our churches. It's understandable, because we are grateful for the sacrifice of our Savior on that cross, but it's regrettable, because we must never forget the ugliness of the cross. It was the most obscene moment in history. It was vile and heinous beyond description. Our precious Lord was hung up naked like a bleeding piece of meat, exposed for all to spit upon and laugh at. It was on a hill; all could see the degradation. He had to endure the most severe mockery and humiliation. Many saints throughout the pages of history have endured such raw torture and humiliation.

However, what no one has had to bear was the ultimate moment of travesty and tragedy that took place when He screamed, "My God, My God. Why hast thou forsaken Me?"

God the Father did forsake Him. He turned His back on His own Son as He was defiled with every sin of every person from Adam to the last man alive. "For God made Christ, who never sinned, to become sin itself." (II Cor. 5:21) He became foul, thoroughly polluted, contaminated and utterly wretched before His Father. It is a price I will never have to pay, no matter how difficult my cross seems to be. But I can never forget what happened there – for me – and for every lost person.

Drawing near to the heart of God will bring the piercing pain of the cross to my own heart; I will sense the shame of the cross. I will see the great price paid for me and others on that cruel cross. It's not a pretty piece of jewelry; it's the instrument of torture that cost God everything to redeem His lost creation. When I see Calvary, the Place of the Skull, as the hill was called, I am motivated. I want to hold dear every drop of blood that fell that day and see it applied to as many hearts as possible. I am ready to let my tinny, earthly reputation go, and wander the hills among the wolves and barbed wire and look for lost sheep. If I get close to Him, He will take me out in those dangerous hills seeking and loving the lost.

The crowds around us will never look the same. We will look through His eyes and see what he saw:

> When he saw the crowds, he had compassion on them because they were confused and helpless, like sheep without a shepherd. (Matt. 9:36)

When we look through our own eyes, we will tire of the brokenness of the human condition. We will become weary with the hard heartedness of the crowds. Their rejection and rebellion will discourage us. But looking through His eyes will be lasting, for His compassion has no end. The great preacher, Charles Spurgeon, said it this way:

> *He who would know love, let him retire to Calvary and see the Man of sorrows die.*

JUST ONE SMOOTH STONE

Just one? I thought we had eight. I thought David had five. That's true. But it only took ONE stone to bring Goliath down.

David never used the rest of his stones, even though they were in his bag. It only took one. And it really only takes ONE to bring down the giant of Religion in our lives. The rest of the stones - Knowing God as a Person, Getting Real, Repentance, Perseverance, Suffering, Obedience and Love for the Lost are all important stones. However, mark this: *All will be fulfilled if we use the first stone well* - TIME. If we spend time alone with the Lord, shut away from the world, sharing everything on our hearts and listening to His, all the rest of the stones will be in our bag. They will just be there - a result of serious, dedicated time given to God.

Chapter Six

JESUS SAYS, "BEWARE"

"Watch out!" Jesus warned them. "Beware of the yeast of the Pharisees and Sadducees."(Matt. 16:6)

This warning is recorded an amazing six times in the Gospels. Admittedly, there are duplicate accounts, but for the Holy Spirit to ensure that this warning was in the text six times, tells us to indeed, BEWARE! The yeast or leaven of both the Pharisees and Sadducees was apparently very toxic and should carry a large skull and crossbones on the label. We wish it was that easy, but yeast or leaven cannot be seen.

My mother asked me to go with her one day to a frame shop. She had the painting with her and needed only to choose the right frame. It was a very small shop but I found the number of choices was overwhelming. The gal at the shop showed her a seemingly endless number of frame options, from large ornate wooden to small metal, and everything in between. Finally, a choice was made and I thought we were leaving. But then a choice had to be made about the border mat to compliment the picture. Together, they looked at every color in the painting, and went through endless possibilities of mat colors. The shop owner could sense my impatience, so she carefully explained to me that it is important to make the right decision, because the mat and frame will make the picture literally "pop out" if it's done correctly.

Galatians 4:4 tells us that when the time was right God sent His Son to earth to live and walk among us. God chose a certain time and set of circumstances, a particular well-chosen frame and mat, to show His Son to the world, and record it all in His Word. The time and circumstance provided the perfect frame to make the true character of God "pop out" against the background. The Pharisees and Sadducees had been around for centuries, but under Roman occupation, they became powerful religious groups that dominated the Jewish culture. Religion was codified and organized with entire books of additional precepts, rules, maxims, formulas and instructions. It would form the absolutely perfect frame and mat for the only begotten Son of God to reveal the Father.

God could have chosen other frame and mat combinations. Jesus could have been set against the business culture of His day, or the Roman officials, or the working folks of that day. And all of them certainly played a part, but the frame in which God chose to reveal His Son was Religion. Jesus bantered back and forth with the Pharisees, scribes, lawyers and Sadducees more than anyone else; and they were Religion personified. After showing us the sharp contrast, He left us with —- "beware"!

What is interesting is that the Pharisees and Sadducees were vehemently opposed to each other. They were two distinct brands of Religion. The Pharisees were very strict about the Word of God. In fact, Jesus commended them as leaders who correctly taught the Old Testament, specifically Moses which refers to the first five books. (Matt 23:1-3) Their doctrine was straight, but they laid aside the weightier matters of the law such as judgment, mercy and faith.(Matt. 23:23) They also concentrated on their outward appearance, with ornate robes and leather boxes tied to their bodies, which contained prayers and Scriptures. Jesus told them they were diligent to clean only the outside of the cup, but left the inside dirty. (Matt. 23:25)

On the other hand, the Sadducees were a loosely connected group until they opposed the Pharisees. They were less strict about interpretation of the Scriptures, and disliked the outward adorning of flowing robes and prayer boxes. They were more connected to the people, and were not so quick to judge and condemn. However, both are under the admonition by Jesus, "beware".

I am not a Religion detective. I am not enlisting others to be Religion detectives or vigilantes. Many people have become aware of Religion and its toxic effects on and in the Church. However, looking for and trying to detect Religion only does what the Sadducees did: it creates another Religion! One group may say pews are Religious, so we will use chairs; one group may say certain buildings are Religious so we meet in an office building; one group may say Sunday is Religious so we will have church on Friday night; one group may say nice clothes are Religious so we wear jeans. All of this has nothing to do with Religion. Religion is a matter of the heart; and fighting Religion will only create more — RELIGION.

I was miraculously born again during what has been called the Jesus Movement in 1970. I became part of a great work of God where many young people were giving their lives to the Lord and receiving Biblically sound training for ministry. Lives were truly transformed and many were sent forth into the harvest fields of the Lord. Many are still in ministry today. But we were infected with Pharisee-style Religion.

The ministry that provided such rich and sound teaching was also critical of others, demanding and controlling. When I finally left, I ran as fast as I could and began ministering in many different denominations and groups. To my amazement, I found wonderful brothers and sisters everywhere, even in the churches where I had to put on a robe to preach! I had been taught that all those denominations were inferior and had departed from the real Biblical truth. I spent the next few years diligently combing through the Word of God trying to find out what I really believed and the Lord taught me so much. However, I could not let go of my disdain for the Pharisee-style Religion and I let it push me straight into the arms of the Sadducees.

How refreshing my new religious world seemed! Everyone seemed to love everyone;

doctrinal differences were set aside; everyone was accepted; and the pastor was just a nice guy. It took a few years to see it, but finally I realized I was in a scarier religious world than the first one. It was scary because it was all so "nice". My first indication was that I saw that people were not delivered from sin; in fact, living continually with sin in our lives was to be expected. Loving the world and the things of the world was just being human and to teach otherwise was "religious"! Help! I went from the frying pan right into the fire.

All the verses about "walking in the Spirit" and the teachings in Romans, Galatians, Ephesians, etc. about a victorious life were not taught or were minimized. Paul had been a Pharisee and fought their religious bigotry regularly, but he was also doing battle with the other religious version of true Christianity. I saw for the first time why Paul had to write words like these from Romans chapter six:

> **1** Well then, should we keep on
> sinning so that God can show us
> more and more of his wonderful
> grace? **2** Of course not! Since
> we have died to sin, how can we
> continue to live in it? **3** Or have

> you forgotten that when we were joined with Christ Jesus in baptism, we joined him in his death? **4** For we died and were buried with Christ by baptism. And just as Christ was raised from the dead by the glorious power of the Father, now we also may live new lives. **5** Since we have been united with him in his death, we will also be raised to life as he was.**6** We know that our old sinful selves were crucified with Christ so that sin might lose its power in our lives. We are no longer slaves to sin.**7** For when we died with Christ we were set free from the power of sin.

When I was in the Pharisee-style Religion, I was taught we had to work hard to enter into the truth of these verses. If we couldn't achieve it, we were under condemnation by others. In the Sadducee-style Religion these verses were basically some "ideal" and we were not expected to live up to them because we were only human. Working to achieve a walk of holiness was deemed "legalistic". Yikes! The fire and the frying pan both led to bondage.

The teaching that seemed lacking in the Pharisee-style Religion was that if we maintain a strong love Relationship with the Lord, the life in the Spirit will be a *result,* just as fruit is merely a result of water and good soil. We won't work at making it happen; we only have to work at our Relationship. For the Sadducee version, the basic antidote for their weak message is the same: if we cultivate a strong, devoted Relationship with the Lord we won't *want* to sin. We won't *want* the things of the world.

For the Sadducees, the response to the endless battle of fighting to walk in holiness is to not fight at all. For the Pharisees, the response to the endless battle of fighting to walk in holiness is to fight harder. Both are disastrous. Both lead to bondage. Sadly, the roadside shoulders along the Narrow Way are filled with those that have given up. Either they are exhausted from having fought endlessly and failing, or bored from merely attending church and living an unchanged life.

The reason I believe that the Sadducee-style is a little more dangerous is that there is struggle and fight in the Christian life. Paul reveals his serious life of discipline and battle in these verses from I Corinthians chapter nine:

> **26** So I run with purpose in every step. I am not just shadow-boxing. **27** I discipline my body like an athlete, training it to do what it should. Otherwise, I fear that after preaching to others I myself might be disqualified.

The Sadducee-style Religion generates the idea that all struggle is legalistic religion. That concept is toxic and perilous. The New Testament is rife with words like struggle, labor, fight, battle, strive, and run. In 2 Timothy, Paul uses the comparison of a Christian to a soldier:

> **3** Endure suffering along with me, as a good soldier of Christ Jesus. **4** Soldiers don't get tied up in the affairs of civilian life, for then they cannot please the officer who enlisted them.

The Pharisees will repeat verse 4 to really say soldiers *shouldn't* get tied up in the affairs of this life. The Sadducees will honor Paul for his commitment, but say it's not for the average person who has to go to work and raise a family. However, all believers are called to be soldiers, and that call entails work. A soldier trains hard, think and talks differently, and puts his or her life on the line. But Paul puts all the work in proper perspective. It's not because we *shouldn't* get involved with the world, but rather that we want to please the Officer who enlisted us. The call is not to give up on hard work to follow Him, but to make sure we are doing it for the One we love and adore.

Chapter Seven

HOW CAN WE KNOW?

'Beware of the leaven of the Pharisees and Sadducees' is a stern and serious warning. But how are we going to know when ugly Religion begins to creep into our souls? When I was growing up in the Santa Cruz, California area, I used to love to watch the fog creep into the forests of the mountains as it moved in from Monterey Bay. It would move like a giant monster, slowly creeping into every little valley and arroyo, and cover the ridges until the trees were gone. You could watch it from high on Summit Road and see it so clearly. However, as it got closer it was harder to see. Not until the sun was blotted out were you even sure it was going to make it all the way to the summit where you were standing; and so it is with Religion. It creeps into every crack and crevice where the Holy Spirit is not working in vital and fresh ways. When you are far from it you can see it. However, when you are in it, it is undetectable; it's subtle and sneaky stuff.

Is there some kind of litmus test that reveals the presence of Religion? Yes, I believe there is. In a word – it's LOVE. Love kills Religion; love destroys Religion; love dispels the fog of Religion. To see the Lord's perception of love, we must look again at His wonderful words from Mark chapter 12:

> **28** One of the teachers of religious law was standing there listening to the debate. He realized that Jesus had answered well, so he asked, "Of all the commandments, which is the most important?" **29** Jesus replied, "The most important commandment is this: 'Listen, O Israel! The LORD our God is the one and only LORD. **30** And you must love the LORD your God with all your heart, all your soul, all your mind, and all your strength.' **31** The second is equally important: 'Love your neighbor as yourself.' No other commandment is greater than these."

Mr. Religion was confronting the Man of Relationship and sought to corner Him when Jesus launched into the truth behind all that God has to say to mankind; it's all about LOVE.

The premier commandment of all is to love God with all our faculties: heart, mind, soul and strength. We all have an amazing ability to deceive ourselves about how much we love God. Over the years of ministry and talking to thousands, I have heard people in the most rebellious and sinful circumstances declare their love for God. The most extreme was one evening when a group of us traveled to a small town in the mountains of Northern California to walk around and witness to the townspeople about God's offer of salvation. The town had one store and two bars and everyone seemed to be in the bars so we spent the evening there. I spoke to a rather drunken man who sat at the end of the bar by himself, looking very torn up by the sorrows of life. When I spoke to him about the love of God, he pulled his head up, beat on his chest and loudly cried "I love God more than everyone else in this world".

Could he be telling the truth? There is a way to answer this question. When someone loves anybody or anything with all their faculties, it just *has* to show in their lives. If someone loves fishing with all his or her heart, mind, soul and strength it *will* manifest. They will talk fishing, or read fishing magazines, and have equipment in the garage and perhaps a stuffed fish on the wall. It is impossible to love anything with that intensity and not have it reverberate from our lives. If a guy loves his girlfriend with all his faculties, it will show. Calls, texts, gifts, and photos will all reveal that his heart, mind, soul and strength are fully engaged. If, on the other hand, the young man says "I never contact her or help her, but I love her" we rightfully wonder.

I was not able to see beyond the sorrowful man on the barstool. Perhaps he had Bibles and books at his home where he studied God's Word seriously. Perhaps he was faithful to a small group study, and he helped in God's work by taking teenagers camping and guiding them along in their relationship with God. Perhaps he just couldn't look to the Lord that night in his trouble and he went to the bar. I don't know. However, if I had been able to get to know him, I am absolutely sure that his vehement declaration of love for God would be displayed in his life. We would have some doubts if his declared love for God did not manifest itself anywhere in his life. Our choices, our words, and our associations will show what or who we fervently love.

For a season in my life I was consumed in anger and sorrow over some very painful events. If anyone had asked me if I still loved God I would have declared a vehement "yes, of course". However, I realize now that I really loved myself. I loved my sorrow and my sense of self-righteousness as they were more important to me than His way of forgiveness and mercy. I could have left the path of self-deception by comparing my heart to real love as described by God Himself: Love is patient, kind, and keeps no record of wrongs as portrayed in I Corinthians 13. But patient love that keeps no records, no file cabinets or even sticky notes, is contrary to our human nature, especially when we are "right" and they are "wrong". The word right is in quotes because, according to Jesus, we are always wrong, if we don't truly and sincerely love our enemies, and thoroughly forgive everyone.

The real litmus test has now arrived. It is the caboose Jesus attached to the big train when He was asked for one commandment. Jesus had to add this second part because they must go together:

> **31** The second is equally important: 'Love your neighbor

> as yourself.' No other commandment is greater than these."

Notice that Jesus finished by stating "these" as a singular commandment. These two commandments are married and "what God hath joined together let no man put asunder." (Matt. 19:6 KJV)

When I was a young Christian and studied these verses from I John chapter four, I was totally confused:

> **20** If someone says, "I love God," but hates a Christian brother or sister, that person is a liar; for if we don't love people we can see, how can we love God, whom we cannot see? **21** And he has given us this command: Those who love God must also love their Christian brothers and sisters.

To me, the Lord had it backwards. It should read: "We can love God who we cannot see, but how can we possibly love people who we *can* see?" I thought the very reason we can love God is because He is perfect, and the very reason we cannot love people is because we can see how imperfect they are! I kept my confusion to myself and moved along trying to be the best servant of God I could be. However, as I faithfully labored in the Lord's harvest fields, I began to see what that verse was all about.

My love for God was lived out and made complete by my love for all people. It was the litmus test of my love for God. Love for people and love for God are inextricably entwined together; they cannot be separated. It is stated clearly in this verse from I John 4:

> **12** No one has ever seen God. But if we love each other, God lives in us, and his love is brought to full expression in us.

His love is brought into full expression in us! So then we *cannot* love God without loving others and He *cannot* manifest His love to people except through us. It is all tightly bound and welded together.

We still might be able to deceive ourselves by saying things like, *"Well, I love her, I just don't like her."* Or *"Oh yes, I love him, I just don't want to hang out with him."* What if God's love was like that? Yes, He loves us, but he just doesn't <u>really like us</u> or <u>want to be with us</u>. We would be lost. The love He offers and asks us to offer is giving, sacrificial and complete. Such self-serving and loveless statements don't stand up to any descriptions we have of true Biblical love.

Just in case we can still deceive ourselves about how we love everyone, Jesus thoroughly qualifies the love He is talking about in both Matthew and Luke. Matthew 5: 38 – 48 reads:

> **38** "You have heard the law
> that says the punishment must
> match the injury: 'An eye for an
> eye, and a tooth for a tooth.' **39**
> But I say, do not resist an evil
> person! If someone slaps you on
> the right cheek, offer the other
> cheek also.**40** If you are sued
> in court and your shirt is taken
> from you, give your coat, too.**41**
> If a soldier demands that you
> carry his gear for a mile, carry
> it two miles. **42** Give to those
> who ask, and don't turn away
> from those who want to borrow.
> **43** "You have heard the law
> that says, 'Love your neighbor'
> and hate your enemy.**44** But I
> say, love your enemies! Pray for
> those who persecute you! **45** In
> that way, you will be acting as
> true children of your Father in

> heaven. For he gives his sunlight to both the evil and the good, and he sends rain on the just and the unjust alike.**46** If you love only those who love you, what reward is there for that? Even corrupt tax collectors do that much.**47** If you are kind only to your friends, how are you different from anyone else? Even pagans do that.**48** But you are to be perfect, even as your Father in heaven is perfect.

I could, somehow, fumble my way through these verses and try to convince myself I am doing a passable job on what the Lord is saying if it weren't for verse 39. I am in trouble here. There are just some people I want to avoid. One day, I was getting in my car to head to town. I was going to visit with a woman who had been coming to our meetings. I had to tell her about something that she was doing that was offending some other people in the group. I felt prepared to speak to her in a reasonable and loving manner. On my way the Lord spoke to me and said, "You can't talk to her". I asked God why not? And He clearly said, "Because you don't love her". I was stunned and silent for a moment. But then I blurted out, "You are right. I think she is a flake. And she has been a Christian a long time and she should know better than to do what she is doing!" I went home determined to get that bigotry out of my heart and to learn to love the unlovable. After all, in my best moments of honesty I realize that *I am* the consummate unlovable flake in God's eyes.

The passage from Luke chapter 6 makes the uphill journey of love even steeper:

> **27** "But to you who are willing to
> listen, I say, love your enemies!
> Do good to those who hate you.
> **28** Bless those who curse you.
> Pray for those who hurt you.
> **29** If someone slaps you on one
> cheek, offer the other cheek also.
> If someone demands your coat,
> offer your shirt also. **30** Give
> to anyone who asks; and when
> things are taken away from you,
> don't try to get them back. **31**
> Do to others as you would like
> them to do to you. **32** "If you love
> only those who love you, why
> should you get credit for that?
> Even sinners love those who love
> them! **33** And if you do good only

> to those who do good to you, why should you get credit? Even sinners do that much! **34** And if you lend money only to those who can repay you, why should you get credit? Even sinners will lend to other sinners for a full return. **35** "Love your enemies! Do good to them. Lend to them without expecting to be repaid. Then your reward from heaven will be very great, and you will truly be acting as children of the Most High, for he is kind to those who are unthankful and wicked. **36** You must be compassionate, just as your Father is compassionate.

These words might be summarized like this: Love – *really love* – anyone who is, or seems like, an enemy by doing good things for them. Pray blessings upon anyone who slanders you, and earnestly pray to the Lord for those who have hurt you in any way. If they need to hit you to take out their aggressions, let them hit you a second time. If someone steals your coat, give them a shirt to match it. Or if they steal your hoses on the front lawn, see if they want the sprinklers too! If you love and do good things only for your friends and relatives who you trust and who love you, what good is that? All the unbelievers do that much. Should you get any credit from God for acting like an unbeliever? Whatever anyone asks you for, give it to them and never demand it back. Don't lend money with the idea of getting paid back – sinners and unbelievers do this also, and it does not count with God. Love your enemies and lend to them anything they need without ever expecting to be repaid. Then your reward from God will be huge, and you will truly be reflecting the image of God to a hungry and broken world. Be full of the same compassion God has for all people.

These verses spell a certain death for my flesh, my self-world and the safe place where I can be a Christian on my terms: RELIGION. Religion is so awesome. I can sit in my religious tower and stay away from all the mean and flaky people out there; I can calculate my giving and make sure that "my money" will be spent on a good cause; I can love my own group and call it Christian love; I can give money to a homeless shelter and let someone else deal with them; I can go to a nice church where all the people are nice like me; I can greet the people around me at church and never go across the church to comfort or greet a stranger; I can sing words I don't really mean; and I can listen to a sermon and thereby please God. Religion is so safe.

But according to Luke 6 the love of God is not safe at all. The love of God will cause us to love our enemies. We will give away our hearts, our substance, and our comfort zone —- to everyone, for any reason, at any time. It is costly, but one thing is for sure: it is not Religious. Relationship will take us out of the web of Religion, and for the Lord, Relationship with Him is DIRECTLY tied to our relationship with others.

The word "hermit" is from a Latin word that simply meant a desert or solitary place. Many Christians in the fifth and sixth centuries retreated to live in the "hermit" or desert because they were so offended by what was happening in the church. The church had become part of society instead of how it began, with the believers living quite separately from the world and showing a different set of values and lifestyle. It seemed too difficult for many sincere believers to stay in the world and still passionately love God. So they became known as hermits.

For many of us, we would like to 'hermitize' our love for God and keep it disconnected from everything else we do. We want to love

God, but not weep in our prayer closet for our co-workers because of our love for them. We would like to love God, and not have to help our enemies. We would like to love God, and not reach out to flaky people. We would like to love God, and stay safely in our group. We want to have our people, at our table, and hope the Lord didn't mean it when He said:

> **12** Then he turned to his host. "When you put on a luncheon or a banquet," he said, "don't invite your friends, brothers, relatives, and rich neighbors. For they will invite you back, and that will be your only reward. **13** Instead, invite the poor, the crippled, the lame, and the blind. **14** Then at the resurrection of the righteous, God will reward you for inviting those who could not repay you." (Luke 14)

After many years, the church began to form monasteries and convents for seekers. This collective of hermits stayed away from all the degradation in the world. But the hermit movement was, and is, a total failure. Trying to love God WITHOUT loving people and reaching out to enemies and the unlovely is impossible. How can we provide the banquet for the poor and lame if we tuck ourselves away in our safe Religious world?

Apparently, we can deceive ourselves about our love for God. We can say we love God while holding on to Religion, the world, or sin with both hands. But God has not left us without a litmus test to measure the reality of our claims. Do we truly sacrificially love all people, including those who slander and use us? It's a good test. It keeps the fog of Religion from creeping invasively into our souls.

Chapter Eight

The Word "Should" Should Go Away

If our Christian life becomes filled with *'shoulds'*, we must stop and look at our Relationship. If we *should* care for the poor and love our enemies; if we *should* love God more; if we *should* read our Bibles more; if we *should* give more; if we *should* get out of our comfort zone and serve God more fervently; if we *should* more freely share the Word of God with our children and their friends; if we *should* reach out to more people at church; if we *should* prepare a dinner for the lost and lonely; (this paragraph is about to go on for pages!) All *shoulds* in your life need to be given a decent burial, preferably in a concrete tomb, hundreds of feet in the ground.

The new birth experience is the most amazing, supernatural event that has ever happened to you and to me. God's own Spirit has taken up residence in our hearts. The power of God dwells inside of us, and it was this amazing act of God that put to death the world of "should" and launched us into the freedom of desire. "I want to" is glorious liberty. Consider these words from the prophet Ezekiel as he looks down the corridor of time, and sees the New Covenant:

> **26** And I will give you a new heart, and I will put a new spirit in you. I will take out your stony, stubborn heart and give you a tender, responsive heart. **27** And I will put my Spirit in you so that you will follow my decrees and be careful to obey my regulations. (Ez. 36)

The New Testament confirms this promise in Hebrews chapter 10:

> **15** And the Holy Spirit also testifies that this is so. For he says, **16** "This is the new covenant I will make with my people on that day, says the LORD: I will put my laws in their hearts, and I will write them on their minds."

These verses reveal the great transition from Law to Grace, from Old Covenant to New Covenant, from Bondage to Freedom, from Should to Want To —- and from Religion to Relationship.

Consider the word "should" in your relationships with your spouse, friends or children. If you are constantly thinking "I *should* spend time with my wife" or "I *should* play with the kids" or "I *should* call my friend" those relationships are in trouble. All healthy relationships are based on "I want to". When you want to spend time with your spouse, when you want to go out and have some play time with the kids and when you call your friend without ever thinking about it, this is real relationship.

The Holy Spirit living inside of us works somewhat like a homing pigeon. No matter where the pigeon flies, it *wants* to go home. It's not that it *should* go home; the pigeon is empowered with a strong internal drive to go home. The home of the Holy Spirit is with the Father, and once He lives inside of us, the pull and push to go home will always be there, every day, all day, and every minute of every day. We may struggle, resist, and drown out the call through the lusts of our flesh, but the drawing power of the Holy Spirit is relentless. Perhaps the voice and pull of the Holy Spirit will become so dim at times we will need a few strong "*shoulds*" to get us going, but if we don't transition from the Religion of Should into the Relationship of Want To, it will not take us the distance in our journey. Galatians 4 says it this way:

> **5** God sent him (Jesus) to buy freedom for us who were slaves to the law, so that he could adopt us as his very own children.
> **6** And because we are his children, God has sent the Spirit of his Son into our hearts, prompting us to call out, "Abba, Father."

The key word in verse 6 is "prompt". It is the Holy Spirit moving inside of us who will prompt us, drive us, and carry us into the arms of the Father. It is the mission of the Holy Spirit to lead and guide us internally into Relationship.

An amplified version of these verses might read: God sent His Son to purchase our freedom so we would not be slaves to the Law, the Shoulds, or Religion, and He adopted us by sending His Spirit into our hearts. The Dove of God will then prompt us into the waiting arms of the Father, crying "Oh Daddy."

It is a one thing to receive a fabulous personally engraved invitation. It is quite another thing altogether to receive the invitation with a limo to carry us, and with every possible expense and extravagance paid for. God has invited us to enjoy a fabulous, meaningful Relationship with Him, but He has also paid our way to get there. Ours sins are canceled, and the power of His Spirit has been sent to carry us and guide us the whole distance where we can, with joy and assurance, cry "Abba, Father".

CPSIA information can be obtained at www.ICGtesting.com
Printed in the USA
BVOW10s1323190713

326365BV00002B/2/P

9 781626 978461